Amare Nega Wondirad

Challenges and Opportunities of Ecotourism Development

Amare Nega Wondirad

Challenges and Opportunities of Ecotourism Development

Ethiopian Perspective

LAP LAMBERT Academic Publishing

Impressum / Imprint
Bibliografische Information der Deutschen Nationalbibliothek: Die Deutsche Nationalbibliothek verzeichnet diese Publikation in der Deutschen Nationalbibliografie; detaillierte bibliografische Daten sind im Internet über http://dnb.d-nb.de abrufbar.
Alle in diesem Buch genannten Marken und Produktnamen unterliegen warenzeichen-, marken- oder patentrechtlichem Schutz bzw. sind Warenzeichen oder eingetragene Warenzeichen der jeweiligen Inhaber. Die Wiedergabe von Marken, Produktnamen, Gebrauchsnamen, Handelsnamen, Warenbezeichnungen u.s.w. in diesem Werk berechtigt auch ohne besondere Kennzeichnung nicht zu der Annahme, dass solche Namen im Sinne der Warenzeichen- und Markenschutzgesetzgebung als frei zu betrachten wären und daher von jedermann benutzt werden dürften.

Bibliographic information published by the Deutsche Nationalbibliothek: The Deutsche Nationalbibliothek lists this publication in the Deutsche Nationalbibliografie; detailed bibliographic data are available in the Internet at http://dnb.d-nb.de.
Any brand names and product names mentioned in this book are subject to trademark, brand or patent protection and are trademarks or registered trademarks of their respective holders. The use of brand names, product names, common names, trade names, product descriptions etc. even without a particular marking in this works is in no way to be construed to mean that such names may be regarded as unrestricted in respect of trademark and brand protection legislation and could thus be used by anyone.

Coverbild / Cover image: www.ingimage.com

Verlag / Publisher:
LAP LAMBERT Academic Publishing
ist ein Imprint der / is a trademark of
AV Akademikerverlag GmbH & Co. KG
Heinrich-Böcking-Str. 6-8, 66121 Saarbrücken, Deutschland / Germany
Email: info@lap-publishing.com

Herstellung: siehe letzte Seite /
Printed at: see last page
ISBN: 978-3-659-40317-0

Copyright © 2013 AV Akademikerverlag GmbH & Co. KG
Alle Rechte vorbehalten. / All rights reserved. Saarbrücken 2013

Acknowledgements

Two persons were extremely decisive for the successful completion of this project. The first one is my respected supervisor **Professor Lluis Mundet**, who have been giving me very constructive comments and forwarding superb ideas to make the thesis academically acceptable. Dear Professor, moreover, I would like to thank you so much for your unreserved encouragements and collaborations you have been doing in the entire Master Thesis research.

Secondly, **Bethlehem Abebe**, an Instructor in Hawasa University, I thank you very much for your priceless support in distributing and recollecting the questionnaire as well as posting it to Spain, Catalonia. In addition to this, Bethy, truly you deserve a special gratitude for your valuable inputs you contribute during the questionnaire design and for sending fabulous pictures of Wondo Genet I have needed gravely.

In addition to this, I have to say thank you all respondents for spending your precious time in favour of my questionnaire during the survey collection.

Finally, my deepest appreciation goes to all EMTM family including my honourable professors from University of Southern Denmark, University of Ljubljana and University of Girona as well as guest lectures from all corners of the globe for having a life time experience and a wonderful time together with you in the entire EMTM programme.

Table of Contents

Contents **Page**

Chapter One: Introduction ------ 1
   1.1 Introduction ------ 1
   1.2 Rationale of the study ------ 3
   1.3 Statement of the research problem ------ 8
   1.4 Expected contributions ------ 10

Chapter Two: Theoretical Framework ------ 12
2. Tourism and sustainable development ------ 12
   2.1. What is tourism? ------ 12
   2.2. Sustainable Development ------ 14
      2.2.1. The emergence of the concept ------ 14
   2.3. Sustainable Tourism ------ 16
   2.4. Ecotourism, definition of the concept ------ 19
   2.5. Principles and Characteristics of Ecotourism ------ 23
   2.6 Ecotourism in Developing Destinations ------ 24

Chapter Three ------ 29
3. Conceptual Framework ------ 29

Chapter Four ------ 33
4. Presentation of the case ------ 33
4.1 General Overview on Ethiopia's Tourism Sector ------ 33
4.2 Description of the Study site ------ 37

Chapter Five ------ 41

5. Methodology -- 41

5.1 Research paradigm -- 41

5.2 Research methods --- 41

5.3 Limitations -- 42

Chapter Six --- **43**

6. Results, Analysis and Interpretation --- 43

6.1 General Profile of unites of observation (Respondents) ---------------------- 43

6.2 Some general questions on Wondo Genet Tourism --------------------------- 45

6.3 Questions related to the availability of supportive or ancillary

services in Wondo Genet area -- 49

6.4 Questions related to type of tourism most compatible to WG area ------- 57

6.5 Questions pertaining to Opportunities of Ecotourism development in WG area ---- 61

6.6 Questions Related to Challenges of Ecotourism Development in

Wondo Genet (Southern Ethiopia) -- 69

6.7 Questions related to public tourism organizations in WG and its surrounding ------ 80

6.8 Some questions pertinent to hotels and eco-lodges in WG & its vicinity ------------ 85

6.9 Hypothesis verification -- 90

Chapter Seven --- **92**

7. Conclusion, Recommendations and Areas of Further Research ------------------ 92

7.1 Conclusion -- 92

7.2 Recommendations --- 95

7.3 Areas of Further Research -- 98

References

Acronyms

DMOs	Destination Management Organizations
EMT	Estimation Maximization Technique
ECSA	Ethiopian Central Statistical Agency
GDP	Gross Domestic Product
ICT	Information Communication Technology
IUCN	International Union for Conservation of Nature
LDCs	Least Developed Countries
MCT	Ministry of Culture and Tourism (Ethiopian)
MDGs	Millennium Development Goals
NCAP	The Netherlands Climate Assistance Programme
SPSS	Statistical Package for Social Science
SPSS	Statistical Package for Social Sciences
TIES	The International Ecotourism Society
UNCTAD	United Nations Conference on Trade and Development
UNDP	United Nations Development Programme
UNEP	United Nations Environmental Programme
UNESCO	United Nations Educational, Scientific and Cultural Organization
UNWTO	United Nations World Tourism Organization
US$	United States' dollar
WCED	World Commission on Environment and Development
WEF	World Economic Forum
WTTC	World Travel and Tourism Council

Chapter One

Introduction

1.1. Introduction

Tourism is now recognized as being a major economic activity of global significance. The international tourist arrivals have been growing steadily since the emergence of tourism and expected to continue despite economic turbulences and security threats across the world. For instance international tourism arrivals grew by over 4 per cent in 2011 to 980 million according to the United Nations World Tourism Organisation Barometer (March, 2012) and expected to continue in 2012, at somewhat slower rate, yet on the track to reach the milestone one billion mark later this year. According to Rifai, UNWTO Secretary-General, International tourism hit new records in 2011 in spite of the challenging economic conditions contributing directly five per cent of the world's GDP, six per cent of total exports and employing one out of every twelve people in advanced and emerging economies. These figures show only the direct contribution of tourism. The following figure of the UNWTO portrays the trend of international tourist arrivals by region. The figure shows the rapid and continuous growth since 1950 and puts a projection of 1.6 billion by 2020.

Figure 1. International Tourist Arrivals by region and growth trend, 1950-2020

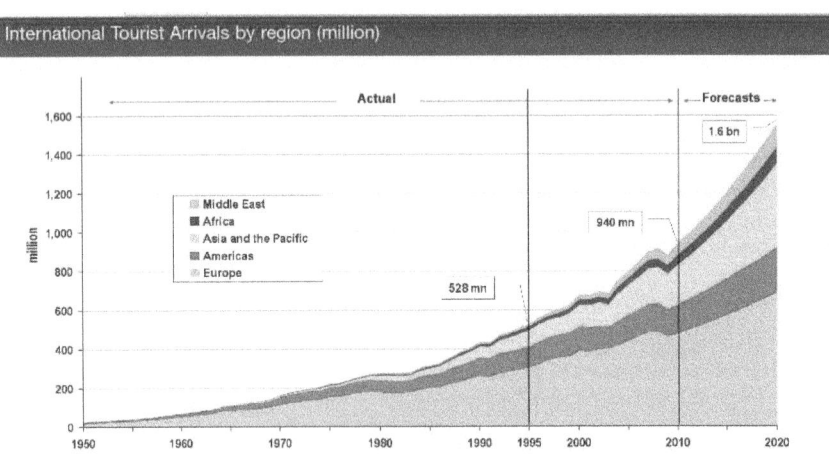

Source: UNWTO Tourism Highlights, 2011

As the importance of tourism as an integrated and diverse activity has increased, so too the attention given to it by governments, organizations in both the public and private sectors, and academics risen (Likorish & Jenkins, 1997). It is an activity requiring inputs of an economic, social, cultural and environmental nature. Nevertheless, as an economic activity tourism has an inevitable effect on the environment of the destination, which is often regarded as the major pull factor of tourist movements, contributing to the desirability and attractiveness of a tourist destination. Since the environment is an indispensable asset to the tourism industry, the protection and conservation of environmental resources including natural, cultural and historic resources are prime considerations for the tourism industry, upon which it depends as primary inputs in the production of the tourist output (Christine & Michael, 2004). Particularly biodiversity and assorted wildlife species are the most valuable compartments of the travel and tourism sector. Due to biological phenomenon, (species richness generally increases with decreasing latitude, Gossling, 1999), the overwhelming majority of species are found in developing countries often faced by multifaceted problems such as rapid population growth, workforce pressure, deforestation, lack of capital and foreign debts, which lead to over-exploitation of wildlife resources, expansion of agriculture and mounting pressure on the remaining habitats and leading to the loss of biodiversity. In contrast, developed countries are characterized by high and increasing demand for nature-based vacations, with protected areas representing first-rate attractions. Tourism could therefore be a means of redistributing economic resources, mitigating the socio-economic situation both at local and national scale, financing infrastructural developments, and contributing to biodiversity conservation.

Therefore, in such a scenario finding an alternative approach of tourism development that conciliates the incongruities among the environmental, economic, and socio-cultural issues is of a profound significance. There is a broad consensus that such tourism should be fully compatible with conservation goals, while at the same time posing a minimum threat to the continuation of local culture and society. Moreover, it should contribute by means of income and education to the conservation of ecosystems. Meeting these requirements would qualify the process as ecotourism (Gossling, 1999: quoted in Brown, et al.).

Ecotourism is the fastest growing portion of tourism and compared to mass tourism, it is heralded as providing better inter-sectoral linkages, reducing economic leakages out of the local economy, paving ways for local communities participation, creating local employment, conserving the ecosystem and fostering sustainable development (Jones, 2005). Thus, it has been popularly promoted as a means of reconciling wildlife and ecosystem conservation with economic development, particularly in developing countries permitting at the same time tourists to enjoy and appreciate nature (Campbell, 1999). Countries such as Costa Rica, a country which has increasingly tailored its industry to fit the ecotourism niche, the Dominican Republic and Belize from the Caribbean and Central America, Brazil, Ecuador, and Peru from South America, Thailand, Cambodia, Laos, and Nepal from South east Asia and Kenya and Swaziland from Africa are some of the fastest growing ecotourism spots in the world (Jeffery, Barclay & Grosvenor, 2012). Ethiopia is an ancient country with one of the richest histories on the African continent, with wealth of castles, palaces, and ancient churches and monasteries as well as unique wildlife, bird life, and breath-taking vistas (Frost & Tekle, 2002). Its wide variety of resources including cultural, natural, historical, archaeological, paleontological and anthropological make Ethiopia the land of extremes and contrasts clearly distinguishing it from other African countries.

However, many developing countries including Ethiopia have not yet fully tapped their tourism resources due to various constraints such as lack of investment in general and tourism infrastructure, presence of non-diversified economic base leading importation of many items which in turn increases economic leakage, unwarranted security atmosphere, poor health and hygiene conditions, transportation inaccessibility and so on. Ethiopia is home to several national parks and protected wildlife sanctuaries which are excellent for ecotourism development. Among them the Wondo Genet area (Southern Ethiopia, have a look on its location map in chapter four) and its vicinity with evergreen protected forest and rich wildlife as well as biodiversity is a best place easily accessible in short distance from the regional hub or capital Hawassa and a reasonable distance from the country's capital Addis Ababa. Yet, although there are numerous opportunities in Wondo Genet area like mentioned above, since Ethiopia is one of the least developed countries there are so many interlinked problems and persistent challenges which require remedies to develop ecotourism on the fundamental assumption that locally participatory, economically viable and environmentally friendly in the destination.

1.2 Rationale of the study

Over the past fifty years, international travel and tourism has shown an extraordinary and fascinating growth. It is now one of the largest and most important industries in the world in terms of employment creation and generation of foreign revenues (UNDP, 2011). Yet, besides employment creation and revenue generation, tourism can also sustain socio-economic development and enhance the quality of life and standard of living of poor nations through financing infrastructural developments, diversifying economic activities, and driving the general economic development through creating interconnections. Indeed the financial contribution of tourism is so massive at global scale. For instance according to UNDP, (2011) data, tourism receipts for 2010 are expected to surpass the $851 billion registered in 2009 with 935 million international tourist arrivals worldwide.

Figure 2. International Tourist Arrivals (million) and Tourism Receipts (US$ billion, 1990-2010)

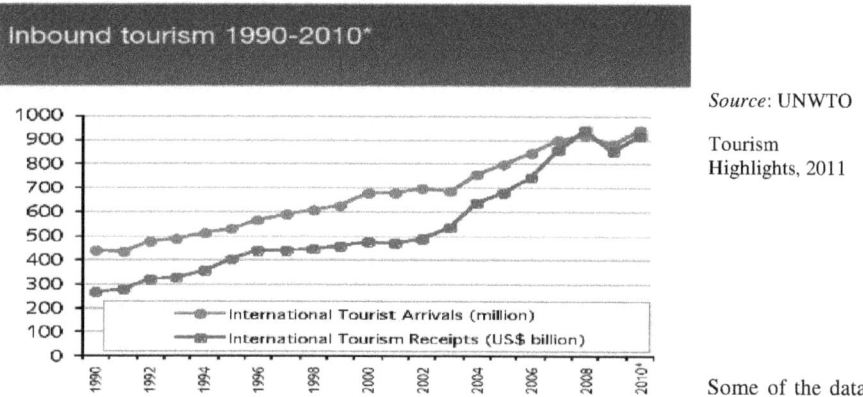

Source: UNWTO Tourism Highlights, 2011

Some of the data of international tourist arrivals and tourism receipts of figure 2 look like the following when transformed in to bar graphs with data labels.

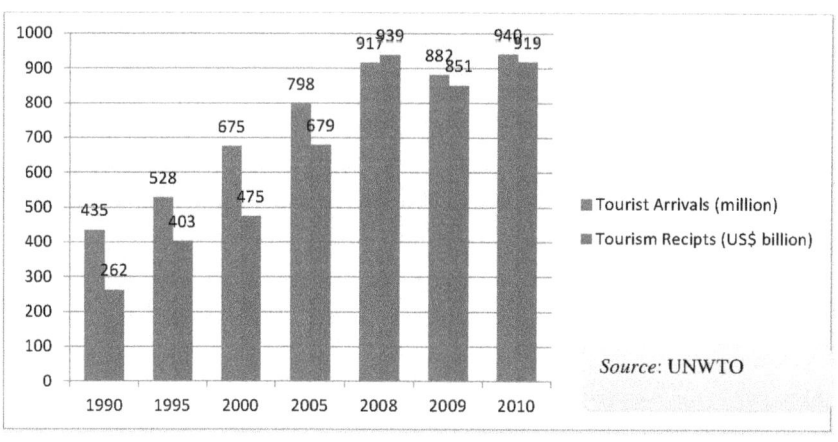

Figure 3. International Tourist Arrivals (million) and Tourism Receipts (US$ billion) with data levels, 1990-2010

Even though it is small compared to well-developed destinations of the world, developing countries have a significant share of this enormous tourism revenue which is so vital for them as a foreign exchange.

Mitchell and Ashley (2010) stated that in 2007 tourists spent US$295 billion in developing countries almost three times larger than the level of official development assistance they get. It is for this reason that tourism has been described as the world's largest voluntary transfer of resources from rich people to the poor people.

However, in spite of its fundamental positive impacts and benefits, tourism can also be damaging and deleterious to a destination through its negative repercussions. Mihalic, (2006) for example stated its negative impacts in detail from the economic, cultural, social and environmental dimensions. Economic leakages, which might be import and/or export leakages, high infrastructural costs, inflation effects, dependency on one economic sector, and seasonal character of tourism are some of negative economic effects whereas commodification, standardization, cultural deterioration, cultural clashes and loss of authenticity are negative cultural outcomes. Moreover, imitations, inequality and hate rate of visitors, social stress, conflicting interest among tourists and residents, crime, prostitution and drug traffickingare among the negative social impacts of tourism. Finally, if tourism is not carefully planned, developed and managed, various negative results on the natural environment such as water pollution, air pollution, noise, visual pollution, littering and waste production, damage to flora and fauna might also occur.

Therefore, sustaining economic growth while ensuring the long-term protection of the socio-cultural and natural environment has been the challenge that the tourism industry has faced. The adverse impacts of tourism are even huge in developing countries due to various interrelated factors. For that reason, in the 1970s and 1980s the notion of searching for a better substitute for the traditional large scale mass and ecologically inimical tourism model has been a subject of discussion and finally has brought the principle of alternative tourism concept in to the sector (Mihalic, 2006). Following the existence of alternative tourism concept, other ideas and thoughts of substitutive tourism forms such as soft tourism, nature based tourism, ecotourism and sustainable tourism have developed.

Even though the degree, scope, weight and effectiveness varies considerably, the bottom line and fundamental reason behind introducing these kinds of tourism development is minimizing the adversative impacts of tourism to the environment, socio-cultural and economic frontages and to capitalize on its positive outcomes.

The concept of ecotourism, which was developed in the 1970s remains still popular in many parts of the world unlike that of soft and alterative tourism. Ecotourism is one compartment of sustainable tourism development firmly based on protecting and conserving fragile and pristine ecosystem, empowering and benefit rural and local communities, promote development in poor areas and destinations, enhance ecological and cultural sensitivity, instil environmental awareness and social conscience in the travel industry, and satisfy tourists through providing quality tourism experiences (Honey, 2008).

Consequently, developing ecotourism seems pretty significant for developing countries like Ethiopia although it is somehow wide-open for "greenwashing" since there is no universally adopted certification program for ecotourism (Self, Hynes & R, Self, 2010). This paves the way for tourism operators to market their operations as "ecotourism" while in reality they are "greenwashing." Yet, the challenges with ecotourism development are much more than just lack of universally approved certification programs particularly in case of developing destinations. On the other hand, there are also several opportunities and prospects which indicate the importance and likelihood of developing tourism in eco-friendly and sustainable manner.

Therefore, the main justifications behind this study, *Challenges and Opportunities of Ecotourism development in Wondo Genet (Southern Ethiopia)*, are:

1. Tourism is not well developed yet in Wondo Genet. So there is the opportunity to develop it in eco-friendly and sustainable way from the grass root level.
2. The area is endowed with various wildlife and ever green forests as well as hot springs with pleasant weather.
3. The local communities in the area are impoverished who would like to get benefit from tourism development.
4. The area is also rich in cultural and traditional attractions such as unique costume, dish, fascinating traditional music and dance as well as special sort of house construction culture.
5. Though it is not so advanced enough, basic infrastructures such as road, telecommunication and some other facilities are already in place.
6. International tourists are already going to the area and knew the place.

7. Most of current Ethiopian holiday makers nearly 90% -(World Bank, 2006) are affluent, well-travelled and well-educated professionals that have been to Africa before who may fit with the characteristics of ecotourists since most of ecotourists are educated, experienced and senior tourists -(TIES, 2006).

In conclusion, deeply studying the prevailing challenges and further identifying future opportunities could help to take better decision and enhance the outcome from tourism by converting all opportunities in to advantages and curbing the challenges which deter its contribution.

1.3 Statement of the Research Problem

"The formulation of a problem is far more often essential than its solution!"

_____ Albert Einstein_____

Currently tourism provides developing countries with major socio-economic opportunities given the labour intensive nature of the industry and the abundance of varied natural and cultural resources in those countries. Tourism is particularly significant for developing nations where the global economy is increasingly driven by sophisticated technologies and service industries causing such poor countries much weaker in the globally competitive market. Therefore, in such a scenario, tourism has become an alternative and highly suitable priority for economic growth and diversification as well as job creation in many developing countries now days due to numerous reasons among which:

- The availability of unique and diverse natural and cultural tourism resources which can draw the attentions of international tourists,
- The capability of tourism to generate job opportunity from semi-skilled to skilled managerial posts as one of the labour intensive industries of the world,
- Since tourism generates valuable foreign exchange and act as an invisible export ,
- Pro-poor benefits to marginalized and impoverished segments of the population including women and youths as well as other income generating opportunities along the value chain that could be created with suppliers and local producers and so on.

Due to these and other many reasons the business of tourism has caught attention of governments, policy makers and private investors as well.

However, tourism has not only economic, socio-cultural and environmental benefits to a certain destination but also detrimental and adverse impacts provided that its development is not managed, controlled and based on the basic principles and concepts of sustainability and eco friendliness.

Consequently, several ideas and concepts such as alternative tourism, nature tourism, soft tourism, responsible tourism, sustainable tourism and ecotourism have been the issues of interest and agenda of debate among various intellectuals, academicians, scholars and authors such as

Adam, (2002), Jacobus et.al(2009), Waver, (2006), Swarbrooke, (1999) and many others in order to stifle the adverse impacts of tourism.

Among the aforementioned concepts of alternative tourism development, the notion of ecotourism has become a pretty interesting concept encompassing forms of travel to a relatively undisturbed and uncontaminated natural areas and exotic cultural destinations as well with the aim of studying, experiencing, admiring and appreciating the natural scenery, wild plants and animals too according to (Jafari et al, 2000). This definition has a close relationship with sustainable tourism development despite it seems quite narrower. Thus, ecotourism is perhaps part and parcel of sustainable tourism development and plays a vital role for the realization of sustainable tourism development as well. As Ross and Wall (1999) attribute, ecotourism is often considered to be a potential strategy to support conservation of natural ecosystems while, at the same time, promoting sustainable local development. However according to the above authors, ecotourism is also defined in many ways in the tourism and environmental literatures and it is being advocated in the absence of widespread recognition of the practical conditions under which it may be best promoted, managed and evaluated. This situation is quite typical in developing destinations due to various reasons among which low level of economic and technological development which preventing them from being able to afford environmental protection measures, techniques and capabilities (Carter, 1993). Furthermore, there are authors (Honey &Gilipin, 2009) demonstrating other obstacles curtailing ecotourism development in third world countries scenarios among which precarious safety and security, poor infrastructural facilities and networks, unsatisfactory health and hygiene statuses, shattered destination image aggravated by the above mentioned factors as well.

Consequently, it is very vital to research about the recurrent challenges which hamper the development of ecotourism and the existing opportunities which could be utilized in developing countries perspective.

Thus, based on the above clarification, this study clearly intended to study about ***the main challenges, potentials and future prospects of ecotourism development in Wondo Genet (Southern Ethiopia).***

Under the major research question, the following issues will be taken in a special emphasis as specific question.

- Is Wondo Genet a proper place for tourism development taking its available tourism resources in to consideration?
- Which types of tourism are more viable to develop in Wondo Genet?
- How can ecotourism be utilized as an instrument towards local sustainable development?

The research will forward its findings to concerned governmental organizations, policy makers and investors regarding challenges and future potentials of ecotourism development in Wondo Genet so that they could have all the necessary information to take an informed decision. Meaning it will identify clearly the main challenges of ecotourism development and future potentials thereby serving as a road map for developing tourism sustainably from the very beginning since tourism in Southern Ethiopia is not well developed so far. That means there is an ample room to go on the responsible and planed way than a haphazard kind of tourism development in the region.

It is also valuable in filling the existing knowledge gap pertaining to the principles of ecotourism development in developing countries perspective.

1.4 Expected Contribution

These days the travel and tourism industry is considered one of the major growing sectors of the globe and a significant factor for economic growth through its direct and indirect effects in the economy and its backward and forward linkages with other sectors of the economy. Furthermore, tourism is considered to be an important instrument of environmental and cultural conservation provided that it is properly developed and sustainably managed. This is especially true for developing countries like Ethiopia which are endowed with various cultural, natural and historical resources, but weak competency in other international markets and transactions. However, most of developing countries including Ethiopia did not take advantage of the abundant endowments and immense tourism resources due to various constraints among which lack of well-trained manpower in the field and inadequate academic studies in travel and tourism industry are the most pertinent.

At this particular juncture, it is possible to say that in Ethiopia general problems and issues related with travel and tourism development deserve a due attention for future developments. In these perspectives this study will have a substantial contribution in detecting and investigating challenges, opportunities and future prospects of ecotourism development in Wondo Genet, Southern Ethiopia.

The outcome will be relevant for taking further actions by governmental organizations, policy makers, non-governmental organizations, private investors and local communities as well. Moreover, it may serve as a corner stone and a reference material for future studies in ecotourism and other related tourism development issues.

Chapter Two

Theoretical Framework

This part of the study has been conducted and presented in order to add relevant know how and an understanding of the selected research problem. Apparently, without reviews of the literature so far have been done, it would be difficult to build a body of accepted knowledge on a given problem identified to be investigated as many authors attribute (Endawoke, et al 2011).

Consequently, relevant books, articles, journals, Master thesis and doctoral dissertations, reports and so on are reviewed in the study as far as theoretical background is concerned.

2. Tourism and Sustainable Development

2.1 What is Tourism?

The definition of tourism differs from source to source and from author to author as well as from institution to institution. So far there is no consensus concerning the definition of tourism. Nearly each and every institution defines the term " tourism" differently. According to the researcher this absence of binding definition of the term tourism might happen because of the complicated characteristics and diverse features of the tourism sector itself.

The first definition of tourism was made by Guyer – Feuler in 1905. Guyer and Feuler defined tourism as "a phenomenon unique to modern time which is dependent on the people's increasing need for a change and relaxing, the wish of recognizing the beauties of nature and art and the belief that nature gives happiness to human beings and which helps nations and communities' approaching to each other thanks to the developments in commerce and industry and the communication and transportation tools becoming excellent." (Esen: quoted in Bahar, 2010).

In their definition of tourism Guyer and Feuler gave more emphasis for issues such as relaxation, necessity for changing environment or place of residence, realization of beauties of nature and art as well as procuring happiness out of what people have visited. They also have indicated what a significance growth in trade and commerce as well as progress in communication and transportation had for the development of tourism industry.

Tourism later was also defined as a collection of activities, services and industries which deliver a travel experience comprising of transportation, accommodation, eating and drinking establishments, retail shops, entertainment businesses and other hospitality services provided for individuals or groups of travellers away from home by Macintosh and Goeldner in (1990).

Still in this definition distinguishing features of modern tourism definition like length of stay issues, domicile matters and the issue of remuneration were not taken in to consideration.

Then after another description of tourism came to in existence by the UNWTO, the leading and biggest international organization in the field of tourism which serves as a global forum for tourism policy issues and practical source of tourism know-how. Consequently, according to this organization tourism has been defined as the activities of persons traveling to and staying in places outside their usual environment for more than twenty-four hours and less than one consecutive year for leisure, business and other purposes which is not related to the exercise of an activity remunerated from within the place visited (Mihalic: quoted in UNWTO, 2006).

So according to this definition, there are three main criteria to label peoples' movement in to the category of tourism. These are;

1. <u>Being away from normal place of residence</u>: the displacement must be culminated outside the usual place of residence. Therefore, a frequent traveller for business or study purposes is excluded from tourism.
2. <u>Type of purpose</u>: the travel must occur for any purpose different from being remunerated from within the place visited.
3. <u>Duration of stay</u>: tourism is not only a travel. It also means or includes staying in a destination. Where the duration of stay is also delimited in between an overnight stay and twelve consecutive months. As a result, tourism is a temporary movement of people to destinations outside their normal places of work and residence.

Goeldner and Ritchie (2009), tried to define tourism in a way that encompasses all the various groups or parties that participate in and are affected by this industry. Based on their definition, tourism is defined as the process, activities and outcomes arising from the relationships and interactions among tourists, tourism suppliers, host governments, host communities and the surrounding environments that are involved in attracting and hosting of visitors.

This definition pretty wider in perspective and scope although it felt to incorporate some basic and founding characteristics of tourism such as purpose of trip and duration of stay like that of the definition given by UNWTO.

To conclude, tourism is a composite of various activities, services, and industries that deliver a travel experience, transportation, accommodations, eating and drinking establishments, shops, entertainment facilities, and other hospitality services available for individuals or groups who are travelling away from home. It consists of all providers of visitor and visitor related services to tourists. Tourism is the entire industry of travel, hotel and transportation and all other components including that of promotion,

From the economic stand point, tourism is the sum total of all tourists expenditures with in the border or a political subdivision of a certain destination.

Finally, Goeldner and Ritchie (2009), attributed clearly that the multidimensional aspects of tourism and its inextricable interactions with other activities caused a problem of coming up with a meaningful and universally accepted definition. This in turn resulted for the existence of various definitions customised at fitting a special situation and solving an immediate problem. Thus, lack of uniform definition has hampered the study of tourism as a discipline since development of a field significantly depends on the existence of uniform definitions, description, analysis, prediction and control.

2.2 Sustainable Development

2.2.1 The emergence of the concept

Now-a-day the word sustainable development has become the "buzzword" of both the academic and the business world. As Paul (2009) articulated, the term "Sustainability" has also been present for the last decades in many academic papers, syllabuses of Faculties, boardrooms of local authorities and corporations and offices of public relations officers. However, sustainability has become a "fashionable" concept in theory, which has been considered extremely expensive to be put in practice by major corporations, firms and local or national governments.

The 1972 Conference on the Human Environment in Stockholm, Sweden, attended by 113 states and representatives from nineteen international organizations, was the first truly international conference devoted exclusively to environmental issues. In that conference experts were able to articulate the connections between environment and development stating that: "although in individual instances there were conflicts between environmental and economic priorities, they were intrinsically two sides of the same coin" Vogler (2007). In addition to articulating the linkage between environment and development, the United Nations Environmental Program (UNEP) was created with a mission "to provide leadership and encourage partnership in caring for the environment by inspiring, informing, and enabling nations and peoples to improve their quality of life without compromising that of future generations.

Despite, the above mentioned contributions the Stockholm conference was limited in its effectiveness because environmental protection and the need for development, especially in developing countries, were seen as competing needs and thus were dealt with in a separate, uncoordinated fashion. As a result, a more integrated perspective that combined both economic development and environmental sensitivities was clearly required. Then, in 1983, the UN General Assembly created the World Commission on Environment and Development which was later known as the Brundtland Commission, named after its Chair, Gro Harlem Brundtland, then Prime Minister of Norway and later head of the World Health Organization. In 1987, the Commission published the Brundtland Report, entitled Our Common Future and the term sustainable development made its first appearance in this report (Mihalic: quoted in WCED, 2006).

Built up on what had been achieved at Stockholm, the Brundtland report provided the most politically significant of all definitions of sustainable development which states as 'sustainable development is development that meets the needs of the present without compromising the ability of future generations to meet their own needs' (Paul, 2009).

The definition comprises two crucial concepts: the first concept is satisfying the needs and desires of the present generation specially the essential needs of the impoverished and secondly thinking about needs and desires of generations to come.

The definition contains two central concepts: firstly, the concept of needs, in particular the essential needs of the world's poor, to whom overriding priority should be given and secondly the idea of limitations imposed by the state of technology and social organization on the environment's ability to meet present and future needs.

But over the years, many new dimensions were added and the concept was redefined, embracing the principles that sustainable development "should be more economically viable, socially just, environmentally appropriate, culturally and ethically conscious, and institutionally effective" (Payne and Raeburn: quoted in Upasana, 2005). On top of that several meetings and discussions (from Bruntland to Rio de Janeiro, 1992, Kyoto, 1997 to New York 2000, Johannesburg 2002 to Copenhagen 2009, and very recently to Durban, 2011). Although leaders and politicians around the world were expected to bring a tangible outcome out of these meetings and conferences, it is possible to say that they failed to reach a common agreement and contribute towards sustainable development. Therefore, in most of the cases on the sole result of many of these conferences and meetings was to increase the carbon footprint rather.

Ramona and Gabriela (2010), in their article named "Relationship between Tourism and Sustainable Development in the European Context", demonstrated that sustainable development is a very dynamic concept with many dimensions and interpretations, seen as a permanent process of change, very connected to the local area needs and priorities.

However, no matter how the concept is dynamic with different dimensions and opened for various explanations, the problem is still the same and the bottom line behind the concept is all about ensuring a sustainable future to the people of the world and to the planet Earth. Yet, realizing this goal requires broad international cooperation, vigilant management of the whole system and process, active political participation, commitment and dedication. In short, all concerned organizations, leaders, politicians, scientists and so on who are involved in the changing of behaviours of individuals and groups in order to contribute to economic growth and development on the basis of sustainable development have to work hard to achieve the objective through active involvement of people.

2.3 Sustainable tourism

A sustainable approach to tourism is based on globally applicable principles of sustainability. Any steps taken toward the management of a destination should be considered in terms of the value of sustainable development. The concept of sustainable tourism development has been derived from the general concept of sustainable development through applying it main principles to the tourism field. Today it becomes a modern and popular concept for making tourism more environmentally friendly and economically viable.

Inskeep (1991), clearly states that the concept of sustainable development explicitly recognizes interdependencies that exist among environmental and economic issues and policies. According to his elaboration, sustainable development is aimed at protecting and enhancing the environment, meeting basic human needs, promoting current and intergenerational equity, and improving the quality of life of all peoples. Inskeep also pointed out that sustainable tourism has the following principal goals of achieving. These are:

- ➤ To develop greater awareness and understanding of the significant contributions that tourism can make to the environment and the economy
- ➤ To promote equity in development
- ➤ To improve the quality of life of the host community
- ➤ To provide a high quality of experience for the tourist or visitor and

> To maintain the quality of the environment on which the forgoing objectives depend

UNWTO (2004) defined sustainable tourism development as "Sustainable tourism development meets the needs of present tourists and host regions while protecting and enhancing opportunity for the future. It is envisaged as leading to management of all resources in such a way that economic, social, and aesthetic needs can be fulfilled while maintaining cultural integrity, essential ecological processes, biological diversity, and life support system."

Thus, sustainable tourism highly emphases and pays special attentions for issues like ecological sustainability, economic viability, and ethical as well as social equitability. Therefore, sustainable tourism integrates the natural, cultural and human environment. It is a kind of tourism development which respects the fragile environmental balance especially in environmentally sensitive areas with a concept of long term developmental perspective.

According to Jamieson (2006), there are considerable imperatives that promote and enhance the vision of sustainability including that of sustainable tourism among which the following could be cited.

> Prudent use of the earth's resources within the limits of planet's caring capacity
> Devolution of top-down decision making responsibilities and capabilities to a broader range of destination's stakeholders
> The abatement of poverty and gender inequalities and respect for fundamental human rights
> Enhancement of the quality of life of residents through improved health care, shelter, nutrition, access to education and income generation skills
> Preservation of biodiversity and life support systems for all natural habitats and
> Preservation of indigenous knowledge and ways of living as well as respect for the spiritual and cultural traditions of different people

Fulfilling these requirements and finding a proper balance different and sometimes conflicting needs and value systems has been the major challenge of realizing the hypothetical explanation of sustainability. Yet, whatever the situation is, sustainable tourism must meet three fundamental and equal objectives which are also termed as three pillars of sustainable development (Mihalic & Jamieson 2006).

These are:

-Economic environment;

- Ensuring viable, long term and efficient economic operation and production of goods and services together with provision and distribution of fair and equitable socio-economic benefits to all stakeholders
- Providing stable, safe and quality employment opportunity, other income generating options and social services to host communities
- Contributing to poverty alleviation in the destination

-Environmental pillar (Natural Environment);

- Conservation and prudent management of natural resources with the preservation of biodiversity and maintenance of ecological integrity as the main conservations
- Sustainable tourism must also maintain a high level of tourist satisfaction besides raising tourists' awareness about environments and promoting responsible tourism practices among them.

-Socio-cultural environment;

- It is all about the maintenance and enhancement of the quality of life (with equity as a main consideration and) intergenerational as well as intragenerational equity in the distribution of wealth.
- It also calls for respecting the socio-cultural authenticity of host communities, conservation of their built and living cultural heritage and traditional values as well as contribution to inter-cultural understanding and tolerance.

Achieving sustainable tourism development requires a strong participation of private sector, community, political leadership and tourists. Waver and Jamieson (2006), pointed out that to achieve sustainable tourism development (Economic profitability as well as environmental sustainability and socio-cultural prosperity), holistic and integrated approach to tourism planning and management should be devised.

It is also well-known that tourism as a sector is a wide and integrated sector involving numerous stakeholders and suppliers. Therefore, making any kind of decision regarding tourism (Sustainable tourism) demands looking in to the broader framework. Among these, allowing communities to better anticipate and prevent problems and make risk- reduced decisions, incorporating the full range of interests and activities in a tourism environment, recognizing the cumulative and synergistic effects of all actions on the ecological integrity of a community and region, identifying the impact of actions on other sectors and other sectors' impact on tourism regions and communities, being aware of the causes and consequences of problems that communities seek to solve, which may involve others and other institutions and understanding the full context of resource use from extraction to end use in the destination are very vital to take in to consideration.

2.4 Ecotourism, definition of the concept

Ecotourism has been widely defined as a form of nature based tourism. Yet, it has also been formulated and studied as a sustainable development tool by non-governmental organizations, academics and various experts since 1990 (Wood, 2002).

Therefore, the term ecotourism encompasses on the one hand to a concept under a set of principles and on the other hand to a specific target market. The first definition of ecotourism was given by the International Ecotourism Society (TIES) in 1990. According to this definition ecotourism is "Responsible travel to natural areas that conserves the environment and improves the welfare of local people" (TIES, Global Ecotourism Fact Sheet, 2006).

Based on this definition, three principal issues are given attention. These are:

- A kind of travel which is responsible,
- A travel is to natural environment with conservation actions, and
- A travel that could improve the wellbeing of the host community

Later International Union for Conservation of Nature (IUCN, here after) defined ecotourism in a relatively broader perspectives and viewpoints. According to this explanation, ecotourism is an environmentally responsible travel and visitation to relatively undisturbed areas in order to enjoy and appreciate nature (and any accompanying cultural features-both past and present) that promotes conservation, with low negative visitor impact, and provides an opportunity for socio-economic benefit and involvement of the local populations (Wood, 2002: quoted in IUCN).

These definitions indicate that ecotourism is a complex phenomenon involving integration of many actors including tourists, resident peoples, suppliers, managers and multiple functions (Ross & Wall, 1999: in Lascurain). It is also possible to envisage that in ecotourism natural environment and local populations are united in a symbiotic relationship through tourism.

Quite recently Singh (2010), defined ecotourism as the management of tourism with the conservation of nature in such a way that the fine balance between the requirements of tourism and ecology on the one hand the needs of the local communities for jobs and new skills on the other hand are maintained to generate income from employment and also keeping in mind a better status for women. In case of Ethiopia, gender issue is of paramount significance and ecotourism might play an important role to open opportunities for side-lined women.

It is clear from this definition that finding the balance between the tourism industry and which includes various actors in it and the host population with their various needs and requirements and reconciling those requirements without compromising the interests and desires of other groups is a challenge of ecotourism development.

Many times ecotourism is viewed as a means of protecting natural areas through the generation of revenues, environmental education and the involvement of local people (in both decisions regarding appropriate developments and associated benefits). This scenario especially is very crucial for developing countries where their share of international tourist arrivals has more than doubled in the last fifteen years and where their touristic destinations are largely unplanned and vulnerable to deep negative environmental impacts.

According to the Quebec Declaration on Ecotourism (2002), though ecotourism embraces the principles of sustainable tourism, the following principles distinguish it from the wider concept of sustainable tourism:

- contributes actively to the conservation of natural and cultural heritage;
- includes local and indigenous communities in its planning, development and operation contributing to their well-being;
- interprets the natural and cultural heritage of the destination to the visitor; and
- Lends itself better to independent travellers, as well as organises tours for small sized groups.

However, Ross and Wall (1999), argued that on the ground distinction between ecotourism and other forms of tourism are often not evident and are widely debated. According to these authors discrepancies are results of the varieties of different perspectives and criteria used to distinguish ecotourism. These include the motivations for imitating ecotourism (e.g. conservation strategy, a business venture, or as part of an environmental education campaign), the motivations of users (are they committed to the conservation ethic or otherwise?), the presence and scale of environmental, social and economic impacts, (e.g. can Yellowstone National Park, US, receiving approximately 3 million visitors per year, and Tangkoko Duasudara Nature Reserve, Indonesia, receiving 2500 tourists annually, both be considered ecotourism destinations?) and the presence and quality of services offered.

It is also quite imperative to think beyond the definition of what ecotourism is and consider about what should be achieved through ecotourism succinctly. In this sand point, Pederesen (1991), briefly demonstrated that alongside providing an enjoyable and enriching experience in nature, the fundamental functions of ecotourism are protection of natural areas, production of revenue, education, local participation and capacity building. Pederesen also added that each of these functions is basic to the overall success of ecotourism and together they can lead to the fulfilment of more specific objectives of ecotourism. This thought seems to be consolidated by Khanal and Babar (2007), as they ascribed ecotourism goes beyond prevailing notions of "the overlap between nature tourism and sustainable tourism" to encompass the social dimensions of productive organisation and environmental conservation. According to their statement, ecotourism does more than create a series of activities to attract visitors, offering them an opportunity to interact with nature in a manner possible to preserve or enhance the special qualities of the site and its flora and fauna, while allowing local inhabitants and future visitors to continue to enjoy these qualities.

Ngunyi (2009: in Ecotourism Australia) defined ecotourism as an ecologically sustainable tourism with a primary focus on experiencing natural areas that fosters environmental and cultural understanding, appreciation and conservation. Regardless of many different sorts of definitions and explanations, there are common grounds behind the term ecotourism in each and every definition. These are the issues of ensuring local communities' participation and benefit out of tourism development, empowering and involving the youths and women, protecting and conserving local culture and the environment as well as ensuring that tourists get quality service and great experience out of their trip.

According to Higham (2007) ecotourism has been compared to many related tourism forms such as nature, farm, wildlife, culture, adventure and so on. Even though ecotourism is somehow related to the abovementioned categories of tourism and can be practiced on farms or in wildlife and consists of adventurous nature to some extent, it also has very unique distinguishing dimensions among which securing local benefits environmentally, economically as well as culturally. Ramser (2007) also elaborated the distinction between ecotourism and nature tourism in a way that ecotourism's main emphasis is on conservation, education, traveller responsibility and active community participation. Finally Higham outlines the positive impacts of ecotourism taking ecological, economic, cultural and social aspects in to account as follows.

Table 1. The positive impacts of the preservation and development of ecotourism

Impact dimensions	Preservation implies	Development implies
Ecological	Conservation & improvement of biosystems	New national parks & zones
Economic	To uphold traditional handicraft Mitigation of seasonality effects	New tourism firms, influx of money
Cultural	Conservation of Heritage sites & Cultures	Restoration of cultural monuments renewed pride in culture
Social	Maintenance of value-systems Preservation of social structures Maintenance of local control	New museums, improvement of infrastructure & social well-being

Source: Higham (2007, p. 40)

2.5. Principles and Characteristics of Ecotourism

So far various definitions, ideas, thoughts and viewpoints about ecotourism given by different authors and scholars of the field have been comprehended. As Higham (2007: cited in Butler, Acott, *et al.*), there are some listed criteria as a basic principles and characteristics of ecotourism. These criteria came out as detailed checklist covering most aspects of the numerous definitions found throughout the literature. Though, Butler's defining criteria of ecotourism seem to be binding in many perspectives, Higham, questions the practical realities of these criteria in many developing countries contexts. Yet, in order to qualify as ecotourism, a certain kind of tourism has to demonstrate the following eight characteristics.

Table 2. Principles and characteristics of ecotourism

1. It must be consistent with a positive environmental ethic, fostering preferred behaviour.
2. It does not denigrate the resource. There is no erosion of resource integrity.
3. It concentrates on intrinsic rather than extrinsic values.
4. It is biocentric rather than homocentric in philosophy, in that an ecotourist accepts nature largely on its terms, rather than significantly transforming the environment for personal convenience.
5. Ecotourism must benefit the resource. The environment must experience a net benefit from the activity, although there are often spin-offs of social, economic, political or scientific benefits.
6. It is first-hand experience with the natural environment.
7. There is, in ecotourism, an expectation of gratification measured in appreciation and education, not in thrill-seeking or physical achievement. These latter elements are consistent with adventure tourism, the other division of natural environment (wild land) tourism.
8. There are high cognitive (informational) and effective (emotional) dimensions to the experience, requiring a high level of preparation from both leaders and participants.

Source: Higham (2007, in Butler, Acott *et al.*)

2.6 Ecotourism in Developing Destinations

In recent years, tourism has been increasingly recognized for its potential to contribute to the reduction of poverty in developing countries (UNWTO, 2001). This is simply because of its wide geographical expansion and labour intensive characteristics in creating many employment opportunities particularly in remote and marginalized rural areas where vast majority of the world's impoverished people live. Dieke (2003) also reinforces the above statement in asserting that many less developed countries (LDCs) now regard tourism as an important and integral part of their economic development strategies mainly because tourism is perceived as a panacea for their fragile economies that are characterized by a scarcity of development resources such as finance and expertise. According to Dieke, these resources are fundamental and needed to increase the economic surplus, without which these countries would be faced to rely solely on international aid to support their developmental efforts. As Higham, (2007 quoted in: Roe et al), tourism is a powerful, potential tool for economic development in lesser developed countries (LDCs) and gross revenues from the tourism industry increased 154 per cent per year from 1990 to 2000 in LDCs, more than double the rate of tourism growth in developed nations. It is the only service sector that provides concrete trading opportunities for all nations regardless of their level of development and it is the number one source of foreign exchange for LDCs, aside from petroleum. Higham also added that 41 of the 50 poorest countries now earning over 10 per cent of their exports from tourism and it is a principal export of 31 of the 49 LDCs and number one for seven of them. Finally, he remarked that these days tourism is in the top five exports for more than 80 per cent of developing countries.

Likewise, UNWTO briefly described the fundamental reasons why tourism is a particularly suitable economic development sector or option for LDCs among which the following could be mentioned.

1. Tourism is consumed at the point of production; the tourist has to go to the destination and spend his/her money there, opening an opportunity for local businesses of all sorts, and allowing local communities to benefit through the informal economy, by selling goods and services directly to visitors;
2. Most LDCs have a comparative advantage in tourism over developed countries. They have assets of enormous value to the tourism industry - culture, art, music, natural landscapes, wildlife and climate, including World Heritage Sites. Visits by tourists to

such sites can generate employment and income for communities as well as helping in the conservation of cultural and natural assets;
3. Tourism is a more diverse industry than many others. It has the potential to support other economic activities, both through providing flexible, part time jobs that can complement other livelihood options, and through creating income throughout a complex supply chain of goods and services;
4. Tourism is labour intensive, which is particularly important in tackling poverty. It also provides a wide range of different employment opportunities especially for women and young people - from the highly skilled to the unskilled – and generally it requires relatively little training;
5. It creates opportunities for many small and micro entrepreneurs, either in the formal or informal economy; it is an industry in which start-up costs and barriers to entry are generally low or can easily be lowered;
6. Tourism provides not only material benefits for the poor but also cultural pride. It creates greater awareness of the natural environment and its economic value, a sense of ownership and reduced vulnerability through diversification of income sources;
7. The infrastructure required by tourism, such as transport and communications, water supply and sanitation, public security, and health services, can also benefit poor communities.

Interestingly, the aforementioned ideas of the UNWTO are further reaffirmed by Honey and Gilpin (2009) and they articulated that, the tourism industry can also help promote peace and stability in developing countries by providing jobs, generating income, diversifying the economy, protecting the environment, and promoting cross-cultural understanding and awareness.

However, though tourism has a multitude of advantages to LDCs from various perspectives as expounded by UNWTO, in order to make sure that the poor and all other concerned stakeholders get equitable share and fair benefit the need to develop tourism in a sustainable and community based manner is very essential. Due to this rudimentary fact, these days many third world countries are turning towards alternative forms of tourism development seemingly benign alternative to uncontrolled mass tourism with its myriads of adverse economic, socio- cultural and environmental impacts.

According to Erlet (1993), most of the defining characteristics of alternative tourism are in direct contrast to those of conventional mass tourism in a way that activities are likely to be in small scale, locally owned, resulting low import leakages and higher proportion of profits retained in the local economy. All these contrast with the large scale, multinational concerns typified by high leakages which characterize mass tourism. Specially, Ecotourism, as a particular variant of alternative tourism, has been eagerly seized upon by Third World destinations as the answer to the classic impasse they find themselves in the need to capitalize on their tourism resources to earn badly needed foreign exchange without, at the same time, destroying those resources and thus compromising sustainability. There are three major reasons for this level of interest as Erlet (1993) attributes. These are:

First, as suggested above, the benefits accruing locally are likely to be greater than those arising from conventional tourism. Second, many Third World destinations have a distinct comparative advantage in attracting ecotourists. They are amongst the last heavens of unspoiled nature and have a wide array of natural assets to attract ecotourists. Thirdly, as the emphasis is on nature, ecotourism in theory should be an ecologically responsible form of tourism in order to ensure that the very resource up on which such tourism is based should be conserved and protected. And so as to warranty the conservation and protection of the natural environment and other tourism resources, better implementation of ecotourism schemes is profoundly crucial. Stem et al. (2003) found out in their case study carried out in Costa Rica that at a large scale, ecotourism may offer significant economic benefits and discourage the conversion of forest to agricultural and pastoral land. Yet, they strongly stress that besides participating and involving the community in income generating activities, increasing the level of environmental awareness and knowledge could ensure greater potential for favourable conservation practices over the long term.

Based on Honey and Gilpin (2009) articulation, ecotourism is a new form of tourism, an umbrella term best defined as responsible travel to natural areas that conserves the environment and improves the well-being of local people stemming from the negative effects of traditional mass tourism to the host environments. Accordingly, a number of countries have tailored their tourism industries adeptly to reflect this desire and have reaped economic rewards while minimizing the environmental and social impacts of growth. Costa Rica led the way in developing the ecotourism concept, closely followed by Ecuador, Tanzania, Kenya, and Nepal. The special report compiled by the above authors, explores the ecotourism model, arguing that if implemented correctly, it can reduce poverty, promote peace and enhance environmental sustainability which are among the Millennium Development Goals (MDGs) of the United Nations. Three countries (Kenya, Nigeria and India) were taken as case studies in order to explore some of the ways in which tourism can enable prosperity, peace and security. Apparently, these countries are developing countries with tourism industries at different stages of development. Kenya has a long-established and successful tourist sector catering to conventional and ecotourism markets where tourism constitutes 2.24 per cent of the national GDP in 2006. On the other hand, in Nigeria, tourism contributes hardly to the national GDP which is 0.02 per cent in 2006. In case of India, even though it is the home for several tourist centres, international receipts from tourism just made up only 0.35 per cent of its gross domestic product in 2006 for example. The outcome from the case studies could be summarized as follows.

In case of Kenya, though development has been uneven, ecotourism has been able to deliver concrete benefits to its people. Since involving local communities is one of its key principles, the admission fees for Kenyans to visit national parks were reduced, providing an important increase to the domestic tourism in the meantime. Furthermore, ordinary Kenyans have been participated in tourism development in their localities and playing a key role in managing and conserving wildlife areas in their own communities. Consequently, tourism has helped employment opportunities and alleviates poverty, the primary United Nations' MDGs. The resilient focus on wildlife conservation and ecotourism also helped Kenya's move toward attaining another MDG which is environmental sustainability.

Unlike Kenya, the story behind Nigeria's tourism industry is incompetent not well organized. Although the country is theoretically tailor-made for tourism with its 370 ethnic groups, various cultural heritages, and also blessed with natural wonders, unique wildlife and favourable climatic condition, yet very little effort has been made at national level to develop tourism. That is perhaps the underline reason why Nigeria failed to establish an official tourist board until 1976 and did not formulated a national tourism policy until the 1990s. Most of its post-independence history also has been understood to the world in the context of political instability, violence, ethnic rivalry and crime. Thus, lack of due attention from the government and absence of strategic planning at national level coupled with precarious peace and security, have been crippling the development of Nigeria's tourism industry.

The case of India somehow looks like that of Nigeria. In spite of its vast size and wealth of natural and cultural tourism resources, India has not been able to turn tourism into a major driver of its economy. Rather than in the country as a whole, tourism only has developed in some pocket areas like Goa, Kerala and the central region around New Delhi. Poor travel infrastructure, poverty, safety and security concerns particularly after the 2008 coordinated Mumbai attacks are some of the stumbling blocks curtaining the Indian tourism industry. On top of that, the national strategy itself has been giving attention only for arrivals and expenditures rather than local involvement and environmental sustainability. Many tourist developments are also owned by outside investors looking toward making quick profit making over that of long term sustainable business operation and ethical business practices. As a result, social problems such as wage exploitation, prostitution and displacement and ecological damage from unplanned and poorly developed tourist resorts, golf courses and amusement parks are the defining characteristics of Indian tourism sector according to the case study conducted.

Consequently, in the vast majority of developing countries challenges like poor travel infrastructural frameworks, especially information communication technology and both ground and air transport infrastructure, lack of capital for further investment, poverty, fragile safety and security, poor health and hygiene, lack of properly trained qualified labour, absence of eminent attention and support from governments, lack of strategic objectives, lack of local community participation and involvement in tourism projects, negative perceptions and poor images by tourist generating countries and so on are the bottlenecks hampering further development of the travel and tourism industry in spite of their immense wealth of natural, cultural and historical tourism resources. On the other hand, intact and pristine natural and cultural attractions, existence of diverse tourist attraction, the growing trend of international tourism to these countries, comparative advantages associated with price competitiveness in almost all of developing countries are some of the bright prospects for the development of tourism in the future.

Chapter Three

3. Conceptual Framework

Tourism has made a significant contribution to the socio-economic development of many countries in the world (UN, 2003). Over the decades, it actually has experienced a continued growth and deepening diversification to become one of the fastest growing economic sectors in the world. Equally, modern tourism is closely related to development and covers growing number of new destinations (UNWTO, 2012). Consequently, while in 1950 the top 15 destinations absorbed 88 per cent of international arrivals, in 1970 the proportion was 75 per cent and 55 per cent in 2010, reflecting the emergence of new destinations, many of them in developing countries indeed. As far as the share in international tourist arrivals is concerned, since the growth has been particularly fast in the world's emerging regions, their share also has steadily risen, from 32 per cent in 1990 to 47 per cent in 2010 (UNWTO, 2012). It looks like the following when it is transformed in to a bar graph.

Figure 3. Tourist shares of LDCs in million in comparison with world tourist arrivals, 1990 & 2010

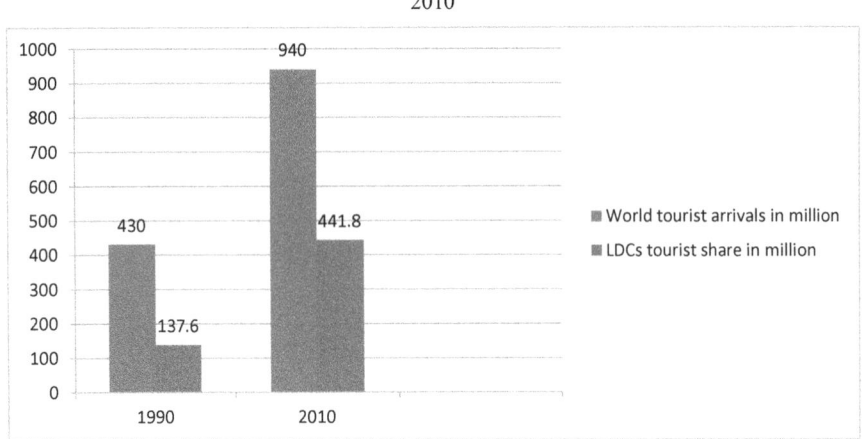

Source: Adapted UNWTO, World Tourism Barometer 2012

These dynamics have turned tourism into a key driver for socio-economic progress especially in those emerging destinations. So, as the world's largest industry, earning approximately $US 2.5 trillion annually (Tiffany, 2000: cited in Dearden) tourism, has a strong potential to be a primary force of influence on the planet. In many scenarios conventionally, tourism has been permitted to develop with little effective planning, regulations and management. For that reason, the tourism industry has created unexpected problems and unwanted effects on the economic, social, cultural and environmental fronts (Ibid). As a result, examining the long-term effects of tourism on the local economy, environment and culture is of paramount significance. Given the above realities, various national governments and the tourism industry itself have become more aware that they must carefully consider how to maintain an intricate balance between the positive impact of tourism and the possible negative effects that can upset plans and goals of sustainability.

Even though, a large controversy exists over its true definition, one class of tourism often cited as a type of tourism which attempts to minimise the negative effects of traditional tourism is ecotourism. Hence, many countries all over the world (E.g. Costa Rica, Brazil, Ecuador, Laos, Kenya etc) have been considering that ecotourism could provide substantial opportunities for future development in ways that highlight their diverse cultural heritage, abundant natural resources and unspoiled environment and eliminate the ill effects of conventional tourism through understanding the cultural and natural history of the destination, maintaining the integrity of the ecosystem and producing economic opportunities for the conservation of natural resources and to benefit local communities. Community-based ecotourism could also be a useful tool for enhancing the standard of living of local people as far as there is appropriate planning and management. Effective conservation and protection of the environment is needed in order to sustain ecotourism. With an emphasis on ecotourism, it is clear that a nation's tourism sector should not be merely a user of natural environment, but should also contribute to its preservation and conservation (Koens, Dieperink, & Miranda, 2009). But yet, there are numerous challenges exceptionally in developing countries which curtail the development of ecotourism from the misuse of the term ecotourism only for as a marketing strategy than implementing its real principles to lack of integrating it in to the mainstream tourism and environmental policies (TIES, 2012), from lack of adequate access to markets to poor infrastructure developments and so on as mentioned in the conceptual framework model below. At the same time, there are also huge potentials and opportunities in these developing countries for the development of ecotourism in the future inter alia existence of massive free land for investment, availability of diverse cultural and natural resources, pristine and unpolluted environmental quality, pleasing weather conditions, growing trend of ecotourists at the international level, for instance, in 2004, ecotourism was growing globally three times faster than the tourism industry as a whole (TIES, 2006) and so on. Therefore, this study or research is related to the above mentioned theories in finding out the challenges and opportunities of ecotourism development in Wondo Genet, Southern Ethiopia since Wondo Genet as a specific destination and Ethiopia in general has intact potentials in the field of ecotourism together with overwhelming challenges which truly demand a due attention from all concerned stakeholders. In conclusion, the following propositions are deducted from the literature reviewed and from the conceptual model seen below.

- Substandard infrastructural developments are acute challenges of ecotourism development in Wondo Genet as developing destination.
- Unorganized and weak institutional framework is one of the important challenges of ecotourism development in Wondo Genet.
- Existence of diverse attractions like pristine natural environments and colourful cultural and historical heritages is a comparative advantage or opportunity of developing destinations.
- Price competitiveness is one of the opportunities for developing ecotourism in Wondo Gent.

```
                    ┌─────────────────┐
    + trends:       │  Tourism in LDCs│      ━━━ Consequences:
                    └─────────────────┘
```

+ trends: (left branch)

Gross revenue from tourism increased by 154% per year from 1990 to 2000,

The only sector with positive trading balance next to petroleum,

41 of the 50 poorest countries now earning over 10 per cent of their exports from tourism,

It is the principal export of 31 of the 49 LDCs and number one for seven of them,

It is also in the top five exports for more than 80% of developing countries.

↓

But, still these LDCs haven't capitalized on their full **potentials** & tourism resources at hand due to various *challenges & restraints*.

↓

-Constraints related to infrastructure

- Tourism infrastructure,
- ICT infrastructure,
- Air & ground transport infrastructure

-Lack of good institutional framework & knowledge management, comprehensive strategic tourism approach,

-Lack of sophisticated promotional & marketing tools,

-Lack of good capacity building & manpower development,

-Absence of proper mechanisms where local communities can participate in various management levels is also a great challenge currently in LDCs.

-Lack of adequate market access

Consequences: (right branch)

Leakages, inflation, acculturation, environmental pollution, pressure & competition on local facilities, local displacement, crimes & prostitution, sexually transmitted & other communicable disease, etc

↓

The way forward for such negative impacts is;

↓

Developing alternative forms of tourism which take all the environmental, social & economic pillars in to account...among which *ecotourism* is widely promoted having unique dimensions to secure local benefits economically, culturally & environmentally.

Opportunities

-Intact & pristine natural & cultural attractions,

-Existence of diverse tourist attraction,

-The growing trend of international tourism & ecotourism to LDCs,

-Price competitiveness of LDCs,

-Ecotourists have a longer stay over than other tourists leading to reduction of carbon foot print etc...

Figure 4. Conceptual model, Adapted from (Christie, 2001, Higham, 2007 & TIES, 2012)

All these challenges are also the acute challenges of ecotourism development in LDCs

Chapter Four

4. Presentation of the study Case

4.1 General Overview on Ethiopia's Tourism Sector

Ethiopia is a landlocked ancient country located in the Eastern Africa Region commonly called the horn of Africa, bordered by Eritrea in the North, Djibouti and Somalia in the East, Kenya in the South and Sudan and South Sudan in the West with a total population of 82.8 million (WEF,2011). It has over 85 ethnic nationalities preserving its own cultural values and traditions for centuries. Christianity and Muslim are the two dominant religions. According to the data obtained from the Central Statistical Agency (CSA) of Ethiopia 2007 (latest available data) 43.5 per cent and of the total population is Orthodox Christian whereas Muslim constitutes 33.9 per cent of the population in terms of religion composition. Protestant and traditional religious group followers accounted for 18.6 per cent and 2.6 per cent respectively. Finally, Catholic and other religions comprised the rest of the percentages. Ethiopia occupies a total area of 1.13 million Km^2 where 7,500 Km^2 is covered by water. High altitude plateaus characterized much of its terrain with its central mountain ranges divided by the Great Rift Valley, and its Westernmost and Easternmost regions constituted altitudes less than 750 meters. Ethiopia is also a country of great geographical diversity and natural contrasts with high and rugged mountains, flat topped plateaus, deep gorges, river valleys and plain areas as well. This diversity in relief makes the country unique in Africa and enables it to have a wide variety of biodiversity. The altitude ranges from the highest peak in Ethiopia (Ras Dashen, 4620 meters above sea level), in Gondar, down to the Danakil depression (120 meters below sea level), one of the lowest dry and hottest places on earth, located in the Northeast part of the country called Afar Regional State (The Netherlands Climate Assistance Programme ,2007).

Figure 5. Map of Ethiopia

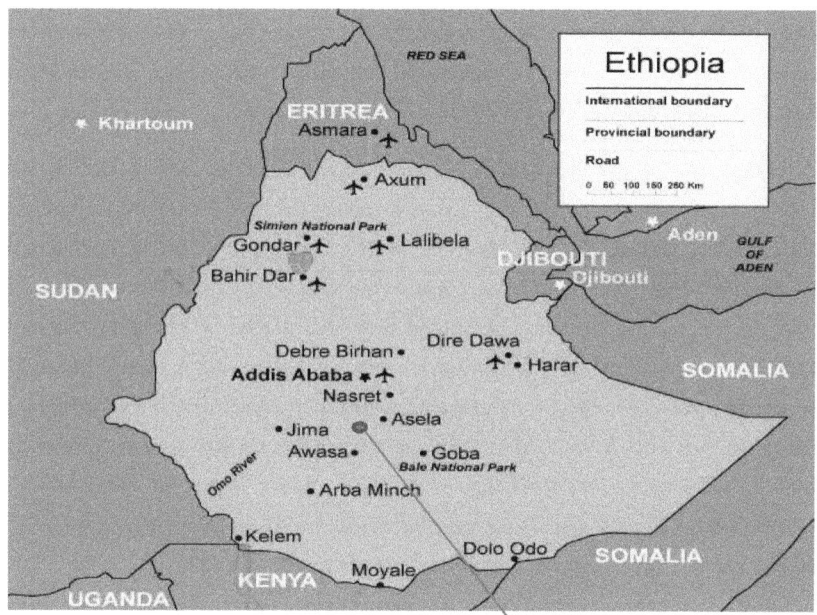

Source: The Netherlands Climate Assistance Programme, 2007

Its closer location to the Middle East and Europe, its pleasing weather, intact cultural and historical attractions, possession of many world heritage sites inscribed under UNESCO and its welcoming and friendly people are some of the competitive advantages that Ethiopia has over other sub-Saharan African countries. Especially due to climatic conditions, Ethiopian tourism season starts in September and reaches its peak in December-January where in those days the Western world experiences a harsh cold winter yet in Ethiopia a clear sky with stunning sunshine which is an ideal weather for holiday makers in those times. Moreover, Ethiopia is a safe country and Addis Ababa is perhaps the only capital city with the seat of the African Union, the United Nations Economic Commissions for Africa and numerous embassies and consulates where you can walk safely at 02:00 AM without fear and danger.

Since its official inauguration as one of the sectors for economic growth in 1965, tourism in Ethiopia has been growing at an average rate of 12 per cent annually which is quite substantial until 1974. Particularly in the four years period, which is between 1970 and 1973, the average number of tourist arrivals to Ethiopia was 63, 833 per year with average annual income of 10.2 million USD (MCT, 2009). However, following the downfall of the late Emperor Haile

Sielassie regime in 1974, the military junta called Derg came in to power for the next seventeen years where tourism in Ethiopia has been declining continuously due to unfavourable conditions created in the country among which prolonged and bloody civil wars, famines created by recurrent drought, cold political and diplomatic relations with tourist generating countries and restrictions to entry and travel within the country can be mentioned.

Nevertheless, after the overthrown of the Marxist Derg regime in 1991, some basic measures and pivotal economic reforms like allowing private investment in travel and tourism, transformation from command economy to free economic system and improvement of foreign relation, elimination of those restrictions to entry and travel within the country etc. have been made. Those reforms and measures had stimulated again the growth of Ethiopian tourism from continuous decline. Since then, tourism in Ethiopia has been growing steadily although it is insignificant compared to the growth of international and regional tourist arrivals. For example, in the four years from 2005 to 2008, the average annual tourist arrivals were 324,664, while average annual revenue was 167 million dollars. Based on these figures, the annual growth rates for those years was projected 21 per cent for tourist arrivals and 19.5 per cent for revenue collected as Ethiopian Ministry of Culture and Tourism stated it in 2009.

UNWTO's current analysis of tourist arrivals places Ethiopia's average annual growth in international tourist arrivals at 5.6 per cent for the period 1990-2000, and at 15.4 per cent during the period 2000-2008. The average growth rates achieved in recent years represent an encouraging trend indeed. The following figure portrays this fact despite the decline after 1974 to the period of its rejuvenation in 1991. One can also noticed an immediate decline in international tourist arrivals and receipts between 1998 and 2000 because of the destructive Ethio-Eritrean war in the period specified.

Figure 6. Tourist arrivals and tourism receipts in Ethiopia, 1963-2005

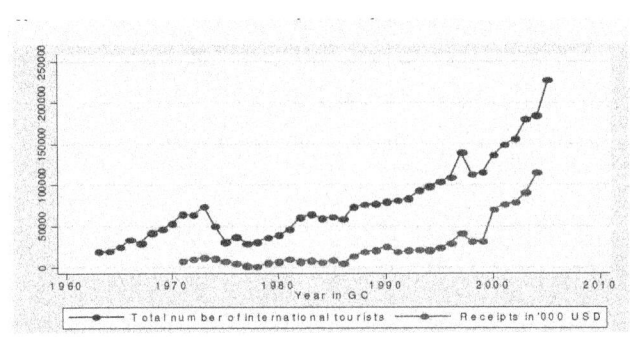

Source: (Yabibal, 2010: in MCT)

Nonetheless, Ethiopia's share of tourist flows compared to the Eastern African Region of seventeen countries in 2007 (the latest available data so far) for example was only 0.7 per cent demonstrating a very low stage of tourism development in the country in spite of its numerous historical, cultural and natural attractions. These days Ethiopian tourism is witnessing a positive trend about 330,000 international tourists visiting the country in 2008 for instance according to the UNWTO (2011). Based on the WTTC travel and tourism economic impact 2012 edition, the direct contribution of travel and tourism to the overall GDPof the countrywas 4.5 per cent in 2011 and is forecasted to grow by 2.4 per cent in 2012. Moreover, the total contribution (meaning the direct, indirect and induced effects) to the GDP in the same year, 2011, looks significant which is 10.8 Per cent with a projected growth by 3 per cent in 2012.

As far as the role of tourism in employment (direct and total) contribution in 2011 is concerned, it has created 909, 500 jobs, which was 3.7 per cent of the total employment directly and 2,271,500 jobs which was 9.3 per cent of the overall employment. According to WEF (2011) travel and tourism competitiveness index, Ethiopia is ranked 122 out of 139 countries, clearly showing how the travel and tourism industry in Ethiopia is lugging behind in the global parameter. Particularly in some pillars such as health and hygiene, tourism infrastructure, Information Communication Technology (ICT) infrastructure, and human resources, it is possible to say that the country is placed at the last frontiers in WEF (2011) travel and tourism competitiveness index. The country has a comparative advantage only in few sub-pillars like carbon dioxide emissions since it is an agrarian country, purchasing power parity, international air transport network and quality of air transport infrastructure, number of world heritage sites both natural and cultural, protected areas and attitude of population toward foreign visitors for example.

Consequently, though it has a positive trend, the Ethiopian tourism currently is highly constrained with numerous acute limitations and sturdy challenges which actually need collaborated and coordinated efforts from the ruling government chiefly and other stakeholders who can affect and be affected by the sector as well. Particularly issues related to health and hygiene (last rank 139), safety and security (102), tourism and ICT infrastructure (128 & 138 respectively) and educating and training of human power deserve a special attention as Ethiopia is in a much worse ranks in these sub-pillars in WEF's 2011 competitiveness index. The environmental performance index of the country in 2010 (141 out of 163 economies) also depicts an utterly poor status demanding a great consideration too. This is because the survival of tourism is hugely depends on the existence of quality environment. Apparently, in principle there will be no leisure and holiday tourism in a degraded and ecologically depleted environment.

4.2 Description of the Study site

Wondo Genet

Figure 7. Map of Wondo Genet in relation to the country's capital & Regional Capital

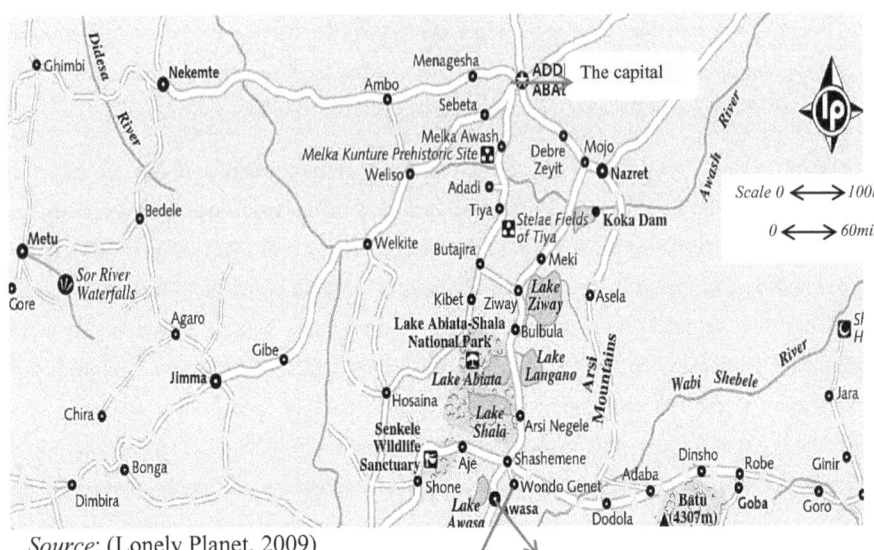

Source: (Lonely Planet, 2009)

Area view 1, Photo: *Bethelhem A., 2012*

Located some 270 Km south of the capital Addis Ababa, Wondo Genet is a well-known destination in Ethiopia especially for its hot springs, lush green dense forest and rich as well as diverse wildlife. It is situated in AwassaZuria district of Sidama Zone within the Southern Nations, Nationalities and People's Region. The area named Wondo Genet, by the then Ethiopian Emperor, Haile Sillassie after using the site for Royal recreational centre since 1971, which literally means a heaven or a paradise place. According to Ali (2007), the Emperor used this term to describe the beautiful panorama of the natural area and its rich endowment of natural resources which include forests, wildlife, magnificent scenic view, ample water flow from streams and springs of fresh water and geothermal hot water as well. Topographically Wondo Genet area comprises the hills of Abaro, BachilGigissa, Gariramo, Kentere and Cheko, and the depression surrounded by these hills. The height of land varies between 2,580 meter above sea level at Abaro and 1,600 meter above sea level around the marshy area (Gemechu, 2005: cited in Belaynesh).

Area view 2, Photo: *Bethelhem A., 2012*

The recreational value and attraction of Wondo Genet is still immensely dependent primarily on its natural endowments and resources. The existence of numerous wildlife species together with attractive landscape scenery, characterize the area as one of tourist attractive destinations in Ethiopia although it has not been well promoted to the international market. As Ali (2007) stated, among the many flora and fauna found in Wondo Genet sub-catchment, it has been shown that 118 bird species, out of which 7 endemic, 3 inter-African migrant and 6 inter- continental migrant species could be observed from part of the sub-catchment though the current status is not clearly known due to lack of updated research. As far as the vegetation species is regarded, Podocarpus falcatus, OleaEuropea, Milliettiaferruginea, JuniperusExcellsa, SyzygiumGuineense, Cordial Africana, Aningeriaadolfi-friedericii, and Prunusafricanus etc are some of the species found of which some are endangered species in the country. Among wild animals, Mountain Nyala, which is becoming locally extinct, Colobus monkey, Anubis baboon and Minellik's Bushbuck, hyenas and leopards are some of the wild animals at the site which visitors may encounter with, of which some of them are endemic species. It is possible to have a look on some of the abovementioned animals and vegetation from the following pictures.

Challenges and Opportunities of Ecotourism Development in Wondo Genet (Southern Ethiopia)

Photos by Bethlehem A., 2012

Legend

- Picture 1...Mountain Nyala
- Picture 2...Columbus Monkey
- Picture 3...Cordial Africana
- Picture 4...Cordial Africana
- Picture 5...Podocarpus falcatus
- Picture 6...Junipers excels

With woinadega (Sub tropical) agro-climatic type, Wondo Genet has a bi-modal rainfall pattern with short rain season between March and May accounting for 28% of total rainfall, and long rain season between July and October accounting for more than 50% of total rainfall. The mean annual rainfall ranges between 700 mm to1400 mm (Cross, 2003). And the mean monthly temperature is 19.5 °C with mean monthly maximum and minimum temperatures of 26.3 °C and 12.4 °C, respectively. Finally, the average annual temperature varies between 17^0C and19^0C Teklay, (2005).

Chapter Five

5. Methodology

5.1 Research paradigm

The paradigm or framework of perception, understanding and belief within which theories and practices are viewed in this particular research is on the basis of interpretivism or constructivism paradigm. As a result, the main goal of the research is to increase the general understanding of the issue which is the challenges and opportunities of ecotourism development in Wondo Genet, Southern Ethiopia. The fundamental reason why this research strategy is applied in this study is due to the fact that ontologically constructivist paradigm considers the existence of multiple socially constructed realities ungoverned by natural laws Lincoln and Guba (2000). Therefore, since the study is a social research, the researcher cannot be completely independent and objective rather part of what he or she is studying under the social constructionist paradigm (Shrestha, 2009). Thus, choosing the constructivist paradigm was more preferable.

5.2 Research methods

Survey is the research method chosen to carry out the study and answer the research question identified. Carefully designed questionnaires (structured questions) as a primary data collection tools and scientific, professional and official articles, journals and tourism research annals, books and so are exhaustively assessed as a secondary data gathering techniques as well. The possibility to collect large amounts of information from a large number of respondents in a relatively short period of time and relatively inexpensive or cost effective way are some of the major reasons to mention why survey method is chosen as a primary data collection technique among others.

The initial questionnaire was subjected to a thorough pre-test using respondents similar to those who will be included in the final survey in order to figure out problems associated with the questionnaire and to have necessary information beforehand how respondents understand questions included as well as to obtain their reflections and comments back on the overall questionnaire. Then, based on the feedbacks obtained from those respondents further clarifications and explanations were made so as to make the final version of the questionnaire fully understandable to all respondents.

The questionnaire, with a total of 69 questions, was subdivided in to eight sub-sections. Consequently, there were subsections focusing on the background of the respondents, general questions, questions related to the availability of ancillary or supportive services, queries pertinent to type of tourism which could be compatible to Wondo Genet area and questions associated to types of specific tourism products that could be developed in Wondo Genet.Moreover, enquiries pertaining to opportunities of ecotourism development in Wondo Genet area, questions concerning to challenges of ecotourism development in Wondo Genet area, questions connected to public tourism organizations in Wondo Genet and its surrounding and questions pertinent to hotels and lodges in Wondo Genet and its vicinity are other categories of the questionnaire survey.

The study population consisted of local people living in Wondo Genet area.As far as the sampling method is regarded, non-probability sampling particularly purposive sampling was applied due to the reason that the notion of ecotourism needs some professional know-how taking the study area in to account. Thus, so as to generate relevant feed backs from respondents, the application of purposive sampling was of a profound importance. University academicians and students, (twelve university teachers and eighteen graduating class students of Hawassa University, Wondo Genet Campus, Department of Wildlife and Ecotourism Management) private business proprietors (ten in numbers) and public tourism organization employees, about ten in numbers, were involved in the sample.

The data collected was analysed through the use of a software package called Statistical Package for Social Sciences (SPSS version 20). The statistical tools used in the interpretation of data and testing of the propositions include frequency counts, weighted arithmetic mean, percentages and mode.

5.3 Limitations

Lack of properly organized and scientifically researched data and information on Ethiopian tourism in general and Ethiopian sustainable, pro poor and ecotourism previous development and current status as well as future projections in particular were the most tenacious constraints in conducting this study. For that reason, Ethiopia was ranked 123 out of 139 countries in comprehensiveness of annual travel and tourism data by (WEF, 2011 travel and tourism competitiveness report). The researcher has tried to fill this gap through researching on other developing countries such as Kenya, Nigeria, Costa Rica and Nepal about issues related to challenges and opportunities of ecotourism development pertinent to developing countries.

Chapter Six

6. Results, Analysis and Interpretation

In this chapter of the thesis, the data collected through questionnaire survey will be analysed and interpreted using statistical package for social sciences (SPSS, version 20). In all cases, missing values of the survey are carefully replaced with predicted values using Estimation Maximization Technique (EMT) of the SPSS which allows the researcher to analyse the complete data set which is more efficient than analysing an incomplete data set. EMT provides the most likely values of some missed items in a questionnaire survey.

6.1 General Profile of unites of observation (Respondents)

Table 6.1.1 Age composition

		Frequency	Per cent	Valid Per cent	Cumulative Per cent
	under 20	2	4.0	4.0	4.0
	20 to 30	43	86.0	86.0	90.0
Valid	31 to 40	4	8.0	8.0	98.0
	41 to 50	1	2.0	2.0	100.0
	Total	50	100.0	100.0	

Source: Author survey, 2012

As the table above shows, the vast majority of the respondents (86 per cent) fall in the age category of 20 to 30. There are only two respondents under the age of twenty and one respondent in the category of 41 to 50. The following bargraph explains the age composition of respondents more precisely displaying the frequency level on it.

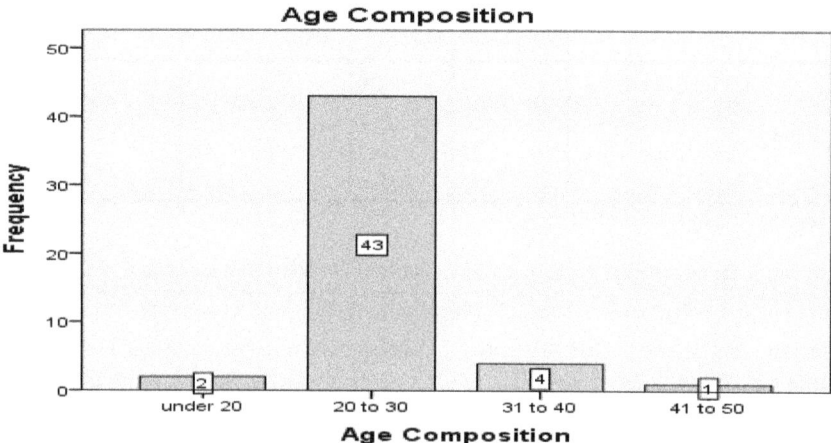

Figure 6.1 Age composition of respondents

Table 6.1.2 Sex composition

		Frequency	Per cent	Valid Per cent
Valid	Female	6	12.0	12.0
	Male	44	88.0	88.0
	Total	50	100.0	100.0

Source: Author survey, 2012

The sex constitution of the respondents depicts that 44 of them or 88 per cent of the respondents are male respondents and 6 out of fifty (12 per cent) of them are female respondents. Since the sampling method used was purposive sampling, the sex ratio of respondents is not evenly distributed and as a matter of fact it was not so relevant to have a consistent sex composition so long as the feedback needed is produced.

Table 6.1.3 Educational profile

		Frequency	Per cent	Valid Per cent	Cumulative Per cent
Valid	College Level	1	2.0	2.0	2.0
	University Degree	37	74.0	74.0	76.0
	Masters and above	12	24.0	24.0	100.0
	Total	50	100.0	100.0	

Source: Author survey, 2012

As far as the educational background of the units of observation is concerned, the data gathered demonestrates that most of them ,37 (74 per cent) of them hold a university degree followed by Master's and beyond holders constituting 24 per cent. The response given could be objective and pertinent since all of the repondents have good educational background as it is shown in the frequency table.

6.2 Some general questions on Wondo Genet Tourism

Table 6.2a Statistics

		6.2.1 Wondo Genet could be regarded as a right place for tourism development mainly from its tourism resource view point.	6.2.2 Length of stay of tourists in WG & its surrounding is short (2 to 3 days)	6.2.3 Safety and security in and around Wondo Genet is strong	6.2.4 Environmental quality & purity of WG and its surroundings is excellent	6.2.5 Wondo Genet is easily accessible to tourists
N	Valid	50	50	50	50	50
	Missing	0	0	0	0	0
Mean		4.7600	3.3400	3.8000	4.5000	4.3800
Mode		5.00	3.00	4.00	5.00	5.00

Source: Author survey, 2012

Table 6.2.1 Wondo Genet could be regarded as a right place for tourism development mainly from its tourism resource view point.

		Frequency	Per cent	Valid Per cent	Cumulative Per cent
Valid	Neutral/don't know	1	2.0	2.0	2.0
	Agree to some extent	10	20.0	20.0	22.0
	Completely agree	39	78.0	78.0	100.0
	Total	50	100.0	100.0	

Source: Author survey, 2012

The above query was provided so as to measure the attitude of respondents regarding the aptness of Wondo Genet for tourism development from its available tourism resource background and as the table displays 78 per cent of them completely agree with the statement specified indicating Wondo Genet is actually the right place for tourism development taking its diverse tourism resource potentials in to consideration.

Table 6. 2.2 Length of stay of tourists in WG & its surrounding is short (2 to 3 days)

		Frequency	Per cent	Valid Per cent	Cumulative Per cent
Valid	Completely disagree	1	2.0	2.0	2.0
	disagree to a certain extent	6	12.0	12.0	14.0
	Don't know/neutral	27	54.0	54.0	68.0
	Agree to some extent	7	14.0	14.0	82.0
	Completely Agree	9	18.0	18.0	100.0
	Total	50	100.0	100.0	

Source: Author survey, 2012

Regarding the length of stay of tourists who have been visiting Wondo Genet and its vicinity, many of the respondents (54 per cent of them) affirmed that they don't have a clear idea on this issue. Yet, 14 per cent and 18 per cent of the respondents stated that they agree to some extent and completely agree respectively that the length of stay of tourists in WG & its surrounding is short (2 to 3 days). The most probable reason why the majority of the respondents replied don't know about the aforementioned issue might be due to absence of scientifically articulated data and lack of academic research about the length of stay of tourists in the area.

Table 6.2. 3 Safety and security in and around Wondo Genet is strong

		Frequency	Per cent	Valid Per cent	Cumulative Per cent
Valid	Completely disagree	2	4.0	4.0	4.0
	disagree to a certain extent	5	10.0	10.0	14.0
	Neutral/Don't know	5	10.0	10.0	24.0
	Agree to some extent	27	54.0	54.0	78.0
	Completely Agree	11	22.0	22.0	100.0
	Total	50	100.0	100.0	

Source: Author survey, 2012

As far as the safety and security in and around Wondo Genet area is concerned, larger segment of the respondents (54 per cent) answered that they agree to some extent that safety and security there is strong followed by 22 per cent expressing that they completely agree with the given statement. Thus, based on the outcome from the survey, it is possible to say that safety and security, which is a vital prerequisite for the existence and survival of tourism, in and around Wondo Genet is strong.

Table 6. 2. 4 Environmental quality & purity of WG and its surroundings is excellent

		Frequency	Per cent	Valid Per cent	Cumulative Per cent
Valid	Don't know	2	4.0	4.0	4.0
	Agree to some extent	21	42.0	42.0	46.0
	Completely Agree	27	54.0	54.0	100.0
	Total	50	100.0	100.0	

Source: Author survey, 2012

The above question was provided in order to discover views of respondents on the environmental quality and purity of Wondo Genet and its surroundings. The outcome shows a positive result where 54 per cent of the respondents marked completely agree alternative followed by 42 per cent who also agree to the statement. As the table above and the graph below show, none of the respondents disagree to the issue. Since environmental quality and cleanliness is one, perhaps the most important constituent of tourism, particularly ecotourism, this quality of Wondo Genet is much more crucial for the development of ecotourism in the area.

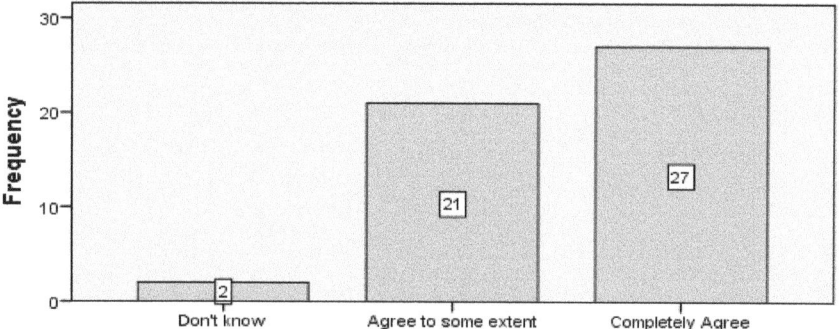

4. Environmental quality & purity of WG and its surroundings is excellent

Figure 6.2 Environmental Quality and Purity of WG and its surroundings

Table 6.2 5 Wondo Genet is easily accessible to tourists

		Frequency	Per cent	Valid Per cent	Cumulative Per cent
Valid	Completely Disagree	1	2.0	2.0	2.0
	Disagree to some extent	2	4.0	4.0	6.0
	Don't know	3	6.0	6.0	12.0
	Agree to some extent	15	30.0	30.0	42.0
	Completely Agree	29	58.0	58.0	100.0
	Total	50	100.0	100.0	

Source: Author survey, 2012

An accessibility question was also provided to respondents in order to find out whether Wondo Genet is easily accessible to tourists and the result above portrays that 58 per cent of them completely agree that Wondo Genet is certainly easily accessible to tourists. Another 30 per cent of the respondents specified their idea that they agree to some extent that Wondo Genet is easily accessible to tourists. Like that of environmental purity and quality, accessibility is also a very determinant factor for the development of tourism in a given destination. From this stand point, Wondo Genet, with its vicinity is easily accessible to tourists.

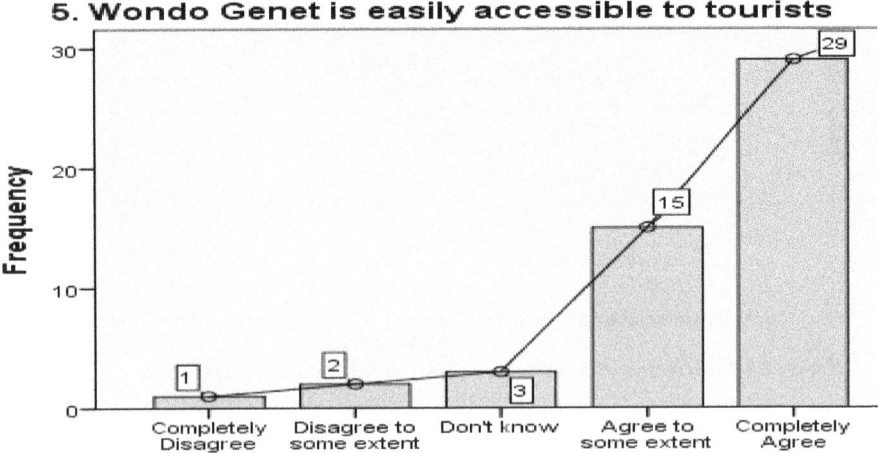
Figure 6.3 Accessibility of Wondo Genet to tourists

6.3 Questions related to the availability of supportive or ancillary services in Wondo Genet area

Table 6.3a Statistics

		6.3.1 There is an elegant banking service in the area	6.3.2 There is adequate and standardized telecommunication service	6.3.3 There is accessibility to clean water	6.3.4 There are adequate shops	6.3.5 There are enough accommodation establishments for tourists
N	Valid	50	50	50	50	50
	Missing	0	0	0	0	0
Mean		2.3200	3.0810	4.3600	2.9200	2.9059
Mode		1.00	4.00	5.00	2.00	4.00

Source: Author survey, 2012

Frequency Tables

Table 6. 3.1 There is an elegant banking service in the area

		Frequency	Per cent	Valid Per cent	Cumulative Per cent
Valid	Completely disagree	20	40.0	40.0	40.0
	Disagree to a certain extent	11	22.0	22.0	62.0
	Neutral	7	14.0	14.0	76.0
	Agree to some extent	7	14.0	14.0	90.0
	Completely agree	5	10.0	10.0	100.0
	Total	50	100.0	100.0	

Source: Author survey, 2012

An important question regarding the functionality of banking services in Wondo Genet was provided to respondents and 40 per cent of them replied that they completely disagree about the existence of elegant banking service whereas 22 per cent of the respondents said that they disagree to a certain extent with the provided avowal. Summing up these two parts produces 62 per cent of the overall responses clearly showing lack of elegant banking services in Wondo Genet, a service which is very indispensable for tourists. The inversion of the above table in to bar graph results the following figure.

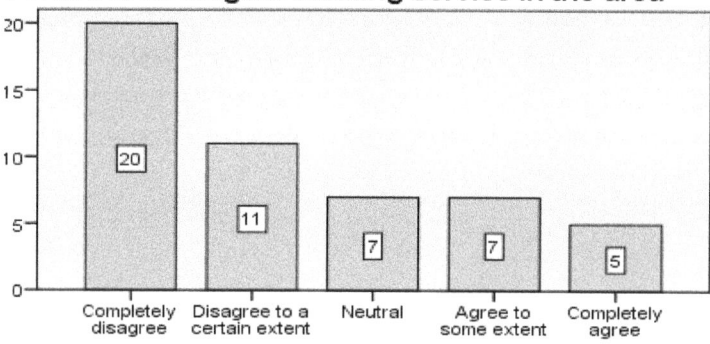

Figure 6.4. The availability of elegant banking service in the area

Table 6.3.2 There is adequate and standardized telecommunication service (like internet, telephone network etc)

		Frequency	Per cent	Valid Per cent	Cumulative Per cent
Valid	Completely disagree	5	10.0	10.0	10.0
	Disagree to some extent	15	30.0	30.0	40.0
	Don't know	5	10.0	10.0	50.0
	3.05	1	2.0	2.0	52.0
	Agree to some extent	19	38.0	38.0	90.0
	Completely agree	5	10.0	10.0	100.0
	Total	50	100.0	100.0	

Source: Author survey, 2012

A query pertaining to telecommunication facility in Wondo Genet was questioned to the respondents and as the table above depicts 19 of them or 38 per cent of the respondents agree to some extent that the is an adequate and standardized telecommunication service. Yet, a considerable amount of the respondents (30 per cent of the total) disagree with the statement to some extent. Ten per cent of them completely disagree and 12 per cent of the respondents neutral to the question. (10% + 2%, i.e. one respondent had left blank this query. However, according to the SPSS's Estimation Maximization Technique (EMT), the maximum possible response of that respondent could be 3.05, where it is possible to approximate it to 3, which is neutral to the given question). Thus, there is a positive indication about the availability of sufficient and standardized telecommunication service in the area which is absolutely very fundamental for tourism stakeholders including tourists.

Table 6.3.3 There is accessibility to clean water

		Frequency	Per cent	Valid Per cent	Cumulative Per cent
Valid	Completely disagree	2	4.0	4.0	4.0
	Disagree to a certain extent	2	4.0	4.0	8.0
	Neutral/Don't know	3	6.0	6.0	14.0
	Agree to some extent	12	24.0	24.0	38.0
	Completely agree	31	62.0	62.0	100.0
	Total	50	100.0	100.0	

Source: Author survey, 2012

As far as the accessibility of clean water is regarded, majority of the respondents (62 per cent) completely agree that there is accessibility to clean water in Wondo Genet. Another 24 per cent of them also agree to some extent that there is accessibility to clean water in Wondo Genet. The availability of clean water in the area is very significant for the development of ecotourism in many perspectives such as investment in Eco lodges, hotels, lodges and so on.

Table 6.3.4 There are adequate shops

		Frequency	Per cent	Valid Per cent	Cumulative Per cent
Valid	Completely disagree	5	10.0	10.0	10.0
	Disagree to some extent	18	36.0	36.0	46.0
	Neutral	7	14.0	14.0	60.0
	Agree to some extent	16	32.0	32.0	92.0
	Completely Agree	4	8.0	8.0	100.0
	Total	50	100.0	100.0	

Source: Author survey, 2012

As the above table portrays, there is lack of adequate shops where tourists might spend in purchasing various goods and items. This condition results in low spending rate per head of tourists negatively affecting the economic contribution of tourism in the area. This is because 36 per cent of the respondents disagree to some extent that there are adequate shops in Wondo Genet. Yet, a significant number of the respondents, (32 Per cent), agree to some extent that there are enough shops for tourists in Wondo Genet.

Table 6.3.5 There are enough accommodation establishments for tourists

		Frequency	Per cent	Valid Per cent	Cumulative Per cent
Valid	Completely disagree	7	14.0	14.0	14.0
	Disagree to some extent	14	28.0	28.0	42.0
	Don't know	8	16.0	16.0	58.0
	3.30	1	2.0	2.0	60.0
	Agree to some extent	17	34.0	34.0	94.0
	Completely agree	3	6.0	6.0	100.0
	Total	50	100.0	100.0	

Source: Author survey, 2012

The above question was provided for respondents in to discover the availability of enough accommodation establishments in Wondo Genet for tourists and as the table exhibits 34 per cent of the respondents agree to some extent that there are enough accommodation establishments in the area while 28 per cent of them disagree to some extent with the statement. Finally, 14 per cent of the respondents declared that they completely disagree about the availability of enough accommodation establishments in Wondo Genet. Summing up these two segments it results 42 per cent disagreeing with the existence of enough accommodation establishments. Consequently, it is possible to say that there is luck of accommodation establishments in Wondo Genet for tourists. This apparently manifests the room for private investment in accommodation services in the area since Wondo Genet has great tourism potentials from its resource perspectives.

Table 6.3b Statistics

		6.3.6 There are community owned enterprises operating & serving for tourists	6.3.7 There are well equipped craft and gift shops	6.3.8. There are enough places to eat and drink	6.3.9 There is lack of entertainment & recreation centre around to extend length of stay	6.3.10 There is lack of restaurants catering traditional & local foods
N	Valid	50	50	50	50	50
	Missing	0	0	0	0	0
Mean		2.7470	2.1444	3.0600	3.0180	3.2706
Mode		3.00	2.00	2.00	4.00	2.00

Source: Author survey, 2012

Table 6.3.6 There are community owned tourism enterprises operating & serving for tourists

		Frequency	Per cent	Valid Per cent	Cumulative Per cent
Valid	Completely disagree	9	18.0	18.0	18.0
	Disagree to some extent	11	22.0	22.0	40.0
	Neutral	17	34.0	34.0	74.0
	3.35	1	2.0	2.0	76.0
	Agree to some extent	8	16.0	16.0	92.0
	Completely agree	4	8.0	8.0	100.0
	Total	50	100.0	100.0	

Source: Author survey, 2012

The above table confirms that 36 per cent of the respondents (34 % +2%) have not idea about the availability of community owned enterprises that operate and serve for tourists in Wondo Genet while 22 per cent of them disagree to some extent about the presence of community owned tourism enterprises operating and catering for tourists. 18 per cent of the respondents completely disagree about the statement, there are community owned tourism enterprises operating and serving for tourists in Wondo Genet area. Only 8 per cent of the respondents completely agree that there are community owned tourism enterprises operating and serving for tourists while 16 per cent of them agree to some extent that there are community owned tourism enterprises operating and serving for tourists in the area. Thus, from the overall responses given above, it could be said that there are not enough number of community owned tourism enterprises operating and serving for tourists in the area. As a result, it might be very essential to organize, and mobilize interested local communities and facilitate, show the way how to establish, own and operate commonly owned tourism enterprises as well as serve for tourists thereby they could be benefited from the development of tourism and the tourism development itself could be pro-poor and sustainable.

Table 6.3.7 There are well equipped craft and gift shops

		Frequency	Per cent	Valid Per cent	Cumulative Per cent
Valid	Completely disagree	15	30.0	30.0	30.0
	Disagree to some extent	19	38.0	38.0	68.0
	2.22	1	2.0	2.0	**70.0**
	Neutral/Don't know	8	16.0	16.0	86.0
	Agree to some extent	7	14.0	14.0	100.0
	Total	50	100.0	100.0	

Source: Author survey, 2012

According to the responses given by the respondents as it is shown on the above table, there is a shortage of well-equipped craft and gift shops in Wondo Genet. 38 per cent of the respondents disagree to some extent that means according to them there are not well-stuffed craft and gift shops in Wondo Genet. Moreover, 30 per cent of them completely disagree with the given statement signifying absence of such establishments. As the cumulative per cent shows generally 70% per cent of the respondents disagree anyway with the statement. (68 % + 2%, since one respondent has not answered this question and this value of 2.22 is figured out using Estimation Maximization Technique of SPSS and should be approximated to 2, which represents disagree to some extent).

Table 6.3.8 There are enough places to eat and drink

		Frequency	Per cent	Valid Per cent	Cumulative Per cent
Valid	Completely disagree	4	8.0	8.0	8.0
	Disagree to some extent	17	34.0	34.0	42.0
	Don't know	7	14.0	14.0	56.0
	Agree to some extent	16	32.0	32.0	88.0
	Completely agree	6	12.0	12.0	100.0
	Total	50	100.0	100.0	

Source: Author survey, 2012

As far as the availability of adequate places to eat and drink is regarded, 34 per cent of the respondents disagree to some extent with the statement supplied by the researcher. On the other hand 32 per cent and 12 per cent of the respondents agree to some extent and completely agree respectively that there are enough places to eat and drink in Wondo Genet. Finally, 14 per cent of the respondents remain neutral about the issue. Therefore, as the feedback from the respondents shows, there ought to be enough places in Wondo Genet to eat and drink. It might be also possible to organize and participate local communities in this arena.

Table 6.3.9 There is lack of entertainment & recreation centre in and around to extend length of stay & increase tourists' expenditures

		Frequency	Per cent	Valid Per cent	Cumulative Per cent
Valid	Completely disagree	13	26.0	26.0	26.0
	Disagree to some extent	6	12.0	12.0	38.0
	2.90	1	2.0	2.0	40.0
	Neutral	5	10.0	10.0	50.0
	Agree to some extent	17	34.0	34.0	84.0
	Completely agree	8	16.0	16.0	100.0
	Total	50	100.0	100.0	

Source: Author survey, 2012

The availability of various entertainment and recreational centres in a destination are very important to extend the length of stay and maximise expenditure of tourists. In this perspective 34 per cent of the respondents agree to some extent that there is lack of such facilities in the area. Other 16 per cent completely agree that there is shortage of entertainment and recreation centre in and around Wondo Genet that help to extend the duration of tourists' stay and increase their expenditures. Therefore, in conclusion, 50 per cent of the respondents (34 %, agree to some extent + 16%, completely agree) articulated that there is lack of entertainment and recreational centres in and around Wondo Genet. Thus, this is also another area of investment opportunity particularly to the private sector there in the area.

6.4 Questions related to type of tourism most compatible to WG area

Table 6.4a Statistics

		6.4.1 Community based ecotourism	6.4.2 Tourism related to cultural or historical attractions	6.4.3 Commercial and recreational tourism (amusement park, golf, resorts)	6.4.4 wellness and health tourism (Spa & thermal therapy related tourism)	6.4.5 Gastronomy (culinary tourism i.e. local food as a product)
N	Valid	50	50	50	50	50
	Missing	0	0	0	0	0
Mean		3.8200	3.6050	3.4043	3.7924	3.1511
Mode		5.00	4.00	4.00	4.00	3.00

Source: Author survey, 2012

As the mean values in the above table represent among the given alternatives, community based ecotourism (with the highest mean value) and wellness and health tourism (Spa and thermal therapy related tourism), with the second highest mean value, are the most prioritised sorts of tourism compatible to Wondo Genet area respectively.

The following Consecutive tables display the attitude of respondents on each alternative provided.

Table 6.4.1 Community based ecotourism

		Frequency	Per cent	Valid Per cent	Cumulative Per cent
Valid	Completely disagree	3	6.0	6.0	6.0
	Disagree to some extent	6	12.0	12.0	18.0
	Neutral/Don't know	7	14.0	14.0	32.0
	Agree to some extent	15	30.0	30.0	62.0
	Completely agree	19	38.0	38.0	100.0
	Total	50	100.0	100.0	

Source: Author survey, 2012

38 per cent of the respondents completely agree that community based ecotourism is very compatible to develop in Wondo Genet and 30 per cent of them agree to some extent about the

statement. Thus, 68 per cent of the respondents agree anyhow about the suitability of community based ecotourism in Wondo Genet.

Table 6.4.2 Tourism related to cultural and historical attractions

		Frequency	Per cent	Valid Per cent	Cumulative Per cent
Valid	Completely disagree	1	2.0	2.0	2.0
	Disagree to a certain extent	9	18.0	18.0	20.0
	2.27	1	2.0	2.0	22.0
	2.81	1	2.0	2.0	24.0
	Neutral/Don't know	7	14.0	14.0	38.0
	Agree to a certain extent	19	38.0	38.0	76.0
	4.16	1	2.0	2.0	78.0
	Completely agree	11	22.0	22.0	100.0
	Total	50	100.0	100.0	

Source: Author survey, 2012

40 per cent (30 % + 2%) of the respondents agree to a certain extent also about the compatibility of tourism related to cultural and historical attractions in Wondo Genet. 22 per cent of the respondents completely agree that tourism related to cultural and historical attractions is appropriate to the area. Nevertheless, 20 per cent of the respondents disagree to some extent about the toning of cultural and historical tourism in Wondo Genet and 16 per cent stay neutral to the issue.

Table 6.4.3 Commercial and recreational tourism (amusement park, golf, resorts)

		Frequency	Per cent	Valid Per cent	Cumulative Per cent
Valid	Completely disagree	4	8.0	8.0	8.0
	Disagree to a certain extent	8	16.0	16.0	24.0
	2.75	1	2.0	2.0	26.0
	Neutral/Don't know	6	12.0	12.0	38.0
	3.68	1	2.0	2.0	40.0
	3.78	1	2.0	2.0	42.0
	Agree to a certain extent	23	46.0	46.0	88.0
	Completely agree	6	12.0	12.0	100.0
	Total	50	100.0	100.0	

Source: Author survey, 2012

As far as the compatibility of commercial and recreational tourism like golf course, amusement parks, and resorts is concerned, 50 per cent of the respondents (46% + 2% +2%) agree to a certain extent indicating such type of tourism is also apposite to Wondo Genet. In addition to this, 12 per cent of them completely agree that commercial and recreational tourism is proper to Wondo Genet.

Table 6.4.4 Wellness and health tourism (Spa & thermal therapy related tourism)

		Frequency	Per cent	Valid Per cent	Cumulative Per cent
Valid	Completely disagree	2	4.0	4.0	4.0
	Disagree to a certain extent	1	2.0	2.0	6.0
	Neutral/Don't know	15	30.0	30.0	36.0
	3.77	1	2.0	2.0	38.0
	3.85	1	2.0	2.0	40.0
	Agree to a certain extent	17	34.0	34.0	74.0
	Completely agree	13	26.0	26.0	100.0
	Total	50	100.0	100.0	

Source: Author survey, 2012

38 per cent of the respondents (34 % + (2%+ 2%, missed values replaced with estimation maximization technique of SPSS, version 20)) agree to some extent that wellness and health tourism like spa and thermal related tourism is compatible to develop in Wondo Genet. Again 26 per cent of the respondents completely agree that tourism related with health and wellness is pertinent to Wondo Genet. Yet, a considerable amount of respondents (30 per cent) have no idea or took a neutral position regarding this statement.

Table 6.4.5 Gastronomy (culinary tourism i.e. local food as a product)

		Frequency	Per cent	Valid Per cent	Cumulative Per cent
Valid	Completely disagree	3	6.0	6.0	6.0
	Disagree to a certain extent	11	22.0	22.0	28.0
	2.76	1	2.0	2.0	30.0
	Neutral/Don't know	15	30.0	30.0	60.0
	3.31	1	2.0	2.0	62.0
	3.48	1	2.0	2.0	64.0
	Agree to a certain extent	12	24.0	24.0	88.0
	Completely agree	6	12.0	12.0	100.0
	Total	50	100.0	100.0	

Source: Author survey, 2012

Gastronomy or culinary tourism, which represents mainly local food items as a tourism product, was also set for respondents to elicit their attitude on this option but unfortunately 34 per cent of (30% + 2% +2%) specified their attitude as neutral to the issue perhaps implying that the idea of culinary tourism is a quite new concept in Ethiopian tourism context and lack of awerness on diversfication of tourism products.

6.5 Questions pertaining to Opportunities of Ecotourism development in WG area

Table 6.5a Statistics

		6.5.1 Supportive rules and regulations from the government	6.5.2 Peace & security (in the country)	6.5.3 Availability of adequate number of trained manpower in the field	6.5.4 Existence of diverse tourist attraction spots and places of special interest
N	Valid	50	50	50	50
	Missing	0	0	0	0
Mean		3.8000	3.6000	4.2600	4.0836
Mode		4.00	3.00	5.00	4.00

Source: Author survey, 2012

Table 6.5.1 Supportive rules and regulations from the government

		Frequency	Per cent	Valid Per cent	Cumulative Per cent
Valid	Completely Disagree	1	2.0	2.0	2.0
	Disagree to some extent	3	6.0	6.0	8.0
	Neutral/ Don't know	13	26.0	26.0	34.0
	Agree to some extent	21	42.0	42.0	76.0
	Completely Agree	12	24.0	24.0	100.0
	Total	50	100.0	100.0	

Source: Author survey, 2012

42 per cent of the respondents agree to some extent that the availability of supportive rules and regulations from the governmental organizations is one of the opportunities for the development of ecotourism in Wondo Genet whereas 26 per cent of them remain neutral to the statement. Another 24 per cent of the respondents completely agree about the given description.

Table 6.5.2 Peace & security (in the country)

		Frequency	Per cent	Valid Per cent	Cumulative Per cent
Valid	Completely Disagree	2	4.0	4.0	4.0
	Disagree to some extent	4	8.0	8.0	12.0
	Neutral/ Don't know	17	34.0	34.0	46.0
	Agree to some extent	16	32.0	32.0	78.0
	Completely Agree	11	22.0	22.0	100.0
	Total	50	100.0	100.0	

Source: Author survey, 2012

As far as the peace and security in the country as an opportunity to develop ecotourism is concerned, 34 per cent of the respondents have taken a neutral stand. Nonthless, another 32 percent and 22 percent of the respondents agree to some extent and completely agree respectively with the issue stated. Therefore, since 56 per cent of the respondents agree anyways, the prevalnce of peace and security in Ethiopia is also an opportunity for the development of ecotourism in Wondo Genet.

Table 6.5.3 Availability of adequate number of trained manpower in the field

		Frequency	Per cent	Valid Per cent	Cumulative Per cent
Valid	Disagree to some extent	5	10.0	10.0	10.0
	Neutral/ Don't know	2	4.0	4.0	14.0
	Agree to some extent	18	36.0	36.0	50.0
	Completely Agree	25	50.0	50.0	100.0
	Total	50	100.0	100.0	

Source: Author survey, 2012

Another very significant opportunity of ecotourism development where 50 per cent of the respondents completely agree with is that the availability of adequate number of trained man power in the field of tourism. So far, there are five public universities and one college together with numerous private colleges offering travel and tourism courses in the country. This circumstance paves the way to produce skilled manpower in the field. Moreover, 36 per cent of the respondents agree to some extent with the existence of adequate number of skilled manpower in the field. Only 10 per cent of them disagree to some extent with the matter declared. Hence, entirely 86 per cent (50% + 36%) of the respondents agree about the presence of trained human power as an opportunity of ecotourism development in Wondo Genet.

Table 6.5.4 Existence of diverse tourist attraction spots and places of special interest

		Frequency	Per cent	Valid Per cent	Cumulative Per cent
Valid	Completely Disagree	1	2.0	2.0	2.0
	Disagree to some extent	1	2.0	2.0	4.0
	Neutral/ Don't know	7	14.0	14.0	18.0
	Agree to some extent	24	48.0	48.0	66.0
	4.18	1	2.0	2.0	68.0
	Completely Agree	16	32.0	32.0	100.0
	Total	50	100.0	100.0	

Source: Author survey, 2012

Existence of diverse tourist attraction spots and places of special interest such as bird watching, sightseeing, culture tours and so on is the nice opportunity of ecotourism development in Wondo Genet according to the attitude of respondents. This is because 50 (48 +2) and 32 per cent of the respondents agree to some extent and completely agree with the subject stated respectively.

Table 6.5b Statistics

		6.5.6 .Existence of hospitable & friendly local population as common to Ethiopia	6.5.7 Existence of natural hot springs which can add value for the normal tourist product	6.5.8 Strategic location in short distance from Hawassa, hub of the regions tourist transition & stopover	6.5.9 The growing trend of international ecotourism demand
N	Valid	50	50	50	50
	Missing	0	0	0	0
Mean		4.5400	4.1800	4.5000	4.2159
Mode		5.00	5.00	5.00	4.00

Source: Author survey, 2012

Table 6.5.5 Existence of hospitable & friendly local population

		Frequency	Per cent	Valid Per cent	Cumulative Per cent
Valid	Disagree to some extent	1	2.0	2.0	2.0
	Neutral/ Don't know	1	2.0	2.0	4.0
	Agree to some extent	18	36.0	36.0	40.0
	Completely Agree	30	60.0	60.0	100.0
	Total	50	100.0	100.0	

Source: Author survey, 2012

As the above table shows, 60 per cent of the respondents completely agree that the existence of hospitable and friendly local population is one of the opportunities of ecotourism development in Wondo Genet. 36 per cent of them also agree to some extent with the given statement. In this perspective Ethiopia as a country has a competitive advantage as it is depicted in the World Economic Forum's 2011 report also. In the sub-pillar of the report termed attitude of population toward foreign visitors, Ethiopia is placed 50th out of 139 countries apparently indicating a competitive advantage. Only one of the respondents disagree to some extent about the provided description and another one remains neutral about it.

Table 6.5.6 Existence of natural hot springs which can add value for the normal tourist products

		Frequency	Per cent	Valid Per cent	Cumulative Per cent
Valid	Completely Disagree	1	2.0	2.0	2.0
	Disagree to some extent	3	6.0	6.0	8.0
	Neutral/ Don't know	5	10.0	10.0	18.0
	Agree to some extent	18	36.0	36.0	54.0
	Completely Agree	23	46.0	46.0	100.0
	Total	50	100.0	100.0	

Source: Author survey, 2012

Natural hot springs found in the area which might add value for the normal tourist products could be taken as opportunities for the development of ecotourism in Wondo Genet area since 46 per cent of the respondents completely agree about it and another 36 per cent of them agree to some extent that the availability of those natural hot springs are the opportunities of ecotourism development.

Table 6.5.7 Strategic location in short distance from Hawassa, hub of the regions tourist transition & stopover

		Frequency	Per cent	Valid Per cent	Cumulative Per cent
Valid	Neutral/ Don't know	2	4.0	4.0	4.0
	Agree to some extent	21	42.0	42.0	46.0
	Completely Agree	27	54.0	54.0	100.0
	Total	50	100.0	100.0	

Source: Author survey, 2012

The above table reveals that 54 per cent of the respondents completely agree that the strategic location of Wondo Genet in close distance from the regional capital, Hawassa is an opportunity for the development of ecotourism in the area. Additionally, 21 of the respondents (42 per cent) agree to some extent concerning the inquiry pointed out.

Table 6.5.8 The growing trend of international ecotourism demand

		Frequency	Per cent	Valid Per cent	Cumulative Per cent
Valid	Disagree to some extent	1	2.0	2.0	2.0
	Neutral/ Don't know	7	14.0	14.0	16.0
	3.79	1	2.0	2.0	18.0
	Agree to some extent	21	42.0	42.0	60.0
	Completely Agree	20	40.0	40.0	100.0
	Total	50	100.0	100.0	

Source: Author survey, 2012

Table 6.5.9 portrays that 44 per cent (2% + 42%) of the respondents agree to some extent that the rising trend of international ecotourism is an opportunity to develop ecotourism in Wondo Genet and 40 per cent of the respondents completely agree about the statement provided. Even though the concept and the issue of ecotourism have begun in 1970s and 1980s, since 1990s, it has been growing 20 to 34 per cent per year. This is a very rapid growth compared to other forms of tourism growth. For instance, in 2004, ecotourism/nature tourism was growing globally three times faster than the tourism industry as a whole (TIES, 2006).

Table 6.5c Statistics

		6.5.10 Weather factor(conducive atmospheric setting)	6.5.11 Tourists profile harmonious to ecotourism & rising arrival trend	6.5.12 Growth of private investors in the travel and tourism sector in the region	6.5.13 Low cost of services and products in the area compared to international market
N	Valid	50	50	50	50
	Missing	0	0	0	0
Mean		3.9600	3.9757	4.3933	3.6688
Mode		4.00	4.00	5.00	4.00

Source: Author survey, 2012

Table 6.5.9 Weather factor(conducive atmospheric setting)

		Frequency	Per cent	Valid Per cent	Cumulative Per cent
Valid	Completely Disagree	1	2.0	2.0	2.0
	Disagree to some extent	3	6.0	6.0	8.0
	Neutral/ Don't know	7	14.0	14.0	22.0
	Agree to some extent	25	50.0	50.0	72.0
	Completely Agree	14	28.0	28.0	100.0
	Total	50	100.0	100.0	

Source: Author survey, 2012

As table 6.5.10 displays 50 per cent of the respondents agree to some extent that conducive atmospheric setting is an opportunity of ecotourism development in Wondo Genet. 28 per cent of them completely agree that weather factor is an opportunity to develop ecotourism there too. 14 per cent of the respondents have not any idea about it.

Table 6.5.10 Profile of ecotourists being harmonious to ecotourism

		Frequency	Per cent	Valid Per cent	Cumulative Per cent
Valid	Disagree to some extent	2	4.0	4.0	4.0
	Neutral/ Don't know	8	16.0	16.0	20.0
	3.79	1	2.0	2.0	22.0
	4.00	1	2.0	2.0	24.0
	Agree to some extent	27	54.0	54.0	78.0
	Completely Agree	11	22.0	22.0	100.0
	Total	50	100.0	100.0	

Source: Author survey, 2012

Another very significant opportunity of ecotourism development in Wondo Genet is the growing tendency of private investors in the travel and tourism sector in the region (Southern Nations, Nationalities and Peoples Regional State). To date there are well organized lodges, resorts, restaurants and hotels in close proximity to Wondo Genet. In aspect of investment, specifically time required to start a business, Ethiopia ranked 35 out of 139 countries in WEF, 2011 competitiveness report. Besides, the government has been incentivising investors in other mechanisms like duty free importation of construction materials, provision of investment land and duty free importation of four-wheel drives for tourist service providers such as travel agents and tour operation companies.

Table 6.5.11 Price competitiveness in the travel & tourism industry

		Frequency	Per cent	Valid Per cent	Cumulative Per cent
Valid	Completely Disagree	2	4.0	4.0	4.0
	Disagree to some extent	4	8.0	8.0	12.0
	Neutral/ Don't know	14	28.0	28.0	40.0
	Agree to some extent	18	36.0	36.0	76.0
	4.43	1	2.0	2.0	78.0
	Completely Agree	10	20.0	20.0	98.0
	5.01	1	2.0	2.0	100.0
	Total	50	100.0	100.0	

Source: Author survey, 2012

As the above table illustrates, 38 per cent of the respondents (36 % + 2%) agree to some extent that price competitiveness in the travel and tourism industry generally at the country level is an opportunity for the development of ecotourism in Wondo Genet. 22 per cent of them (20 % + 2%) completely agree that account provided is an opportunity too. -WEF, 2011 report also placed Ethiopia 23 out of 139 countries in price competitiveness of travel and tourism industry which is a competitive advantage indeed. Yet, a significant number of respondents (28 per cent) stay neutral about the statement perhaps due to lack of information about international price differences.

6.6 Questions Related to Challenges of Ecotourism Development in Wondo Genet (Southern Ethiopia)

In the following part questions pertaining to challenges of ecotourism development in Wondo Genet are analysed and discussed using frequency tables, mean values and modes extracted from the questionnaire survey.

Table 6.6a statistics

		6.6.1 Lack of abundant health facilities in the area	6.6.2 Lack of telecommunication services specially internet banking and internet services	6.6.3 Technological limitations in waste treatment and recycling	6.6.4 Absence of clear guidelines, pushing hoteliers to reduce energy & water consumption	6.6.5 Lack of awareness towards cleaner production & eco-friendly business ethics
N	Valid	50	50	50	50	50
	Missing	0	0	0	0	0
Mean		3.9400	3.8400	3.6185	3.3400	3.3188
Mode		5.00	5.00	5.00	4.00	4.00

Source: Author survey, 2012

Table 6.6.1 Lack of abundant health facilities in the area

		Frequency	Per cent	Valid Per cent	Cumulative Per cent
Valid	Completely Disagree	4	8.0	8.0	8.0
	Disagree to some extent	4	8.0	8.0	16.0
	Neutral/ Don't know	3	6.0	6.0	22.0
	Agree to some extent	19	38.0	38.0	60.0
	Completely Agree	20	40.0	40.0	100.0
	Total	50	100.0	100.0	

Source: Author survey, 2012

The above table illuminates that 40 per cent of the respondents completely agree that shortage of adequate health facilities in the area is the challenge of ecotourism development in Wondo Genet. Furthermore, 38 per cent of the respondents also agree to some extent that the specified statement is one of the challenges of ecotourism development in the area.

Table 6.6.2 Lack of telecommunication services specially internet banking and internet services

		Frequency	Per cent	Valid Per cent	Cumulative Per cent
Valid	Completely Disagree	2	4.0	4.0	4.0
	Disagree to some extent	8	16.0	16.0	20.0
	Neutral/ Don't know	6	12.0	12.0	32.0
	Agree to some extent	14	28.0	28.0	60.0
	Completely Agree	20	40.0	40.0	100.0
	Total	50	100.0	100.0	

Source: Author survey, 2012

Lack of telecommunication services particularly internet banking and internet services is another challenge of ecotourism development since 40 per cent of the respondents completely agree with the statement and another 28 per cent of them agree to some extent about the problem mentioned.

Table 6.6.3 Technological limitation in waste treatment and recycling

		Frequency	Per cent	Valid Per cent	Cumulative Per cent
Valid	Completely Disagree	5	10.0	10.0	10.0
	1.84	1	2.0	2.0	12.0
	Disagree to some extent	5	10.0	10.0	22.0
	Neutral/ Don't know	8	16.0	16.0	38.0
	Agree to some extent	15	30.0	30.0	68.0
	Completely Agree	16	32.0	32.0	100.0
	Total	50	100.0	100.0	

Source: Author survey, 2012

As the above table shows 32 per cent of the respondents completely agree that technological constraint in waste treatment and recycling is the challenge for the development of ecotourism in Wondo Genet. 30 per cent of them also agree to some extent that technological limitation is the challenge for the development of ecotourism in the area. Thirdly, 16 per cent of the respondents have no idea that technological shortcomings as a challenge of ecotourism development in Wondo Genet.

Table 6.6.4 Absence of clear guidelines, pushing hoteliers to reduce energy & water consumption

		Frequency	Per cent	Valid Per cent	Cumulative Per cent
Valid	Completely Disagree	5	10.0	10.0	10.0
	Disagree to some extent	8	16.0	16.0	26.0
	Neutral/ Don't know	11	22.0	22.0	48.0
	Agree to some extent	17	34.0	34.0	82.0
	Completely Agree	9	18.0	18.0	100.0
	Total	50	100.0	100.0	

Source: Author survey, 2012

Table 6.6.5 Lack of awareness towards cleaner production & eco-friendly business ethics

		Frequency	Per cent	Valid Per cent	Cumulative Per cent
Valid	Completely Disagree	7	14.0	14.0	14.0
	Disagree to some extent	8	16.0	16.0	30.0
	Neutral/ Don't know	4	8.0	8.0	38.0
	3.28	1	2.0	2.0	40.0
	Agree to some extent	21	42.0	42.0	82.0
	Completely Agree	9	18.0	18.0	100.0
	Total	50	100.0	100.0	

Source: Author survey, 2012

Based on the above table, 42 per cent of the respondents agree to some extent that lack of awareness about cleaner production and eco-friendly business ethics is one of the challenges of ecotourism development in Wondo Genet and 18 per cent of the respondents completely agree with the given statement. Nevertheless, 16 per cent and 14 per cent of the respondents disagree to some extent and completely disagree respectively that lack of awareness about cleaner production and eco-friendly business ethics is a challenge for ecotourism development in Wondo Genet.

Table 6.6b Statistics

	6.6.6 Absence of strategic policy frame work & environmental code of ethics specifically addressing issues related to ecotourism development	6.6.7 Lack of persistent attention and follow-up about tourism development in general and ecotourism development in particular both at the national and regional level	6.6.8 Lack of strong and sustainable tourism marketing tailored to target markets both at national and regional level	6.6.9 Difficulty of linking & integrating tourism with other local economies	6.6.10 difficulty of creating strong synergy and value chain among various stakeholders that play key roles in the travel and tourism industry
N Valid	50	50	50	50	
Missing	0	0	0	0	
Mean	3.3600	3.4800	3.5400	3.3000	3.6600
Mode	5.00	5.00	5.00	4.00^a	4.00

Source: Author survey, 2012

Table 6.6.6 Absence of strategic policy framework & environmental code of ethics specifically addressing issues related to ecotourism development

		Frequency	Per cent	Valid Per cent	Cumulative Per cent
Valid	Completely Disagree	4	8.0	8.0	8.0
	Disagree to some extent	11	22.0	22.0	30.0
	Neutral/ Don't know	11	22.0	22.0	52.0
	Agree to some extent	11	22.0	22.0	74.0
	Completely Agree	13	26.0	26.0	100.0
	Total	50	100.0	100.0	

Source: Author survey, 2012

Table 6.6.6 exhibits that 26 per cent of the respondents completely agree that absence of policy framework and environmental code of ethics specifically addressing issues related to ecotourism development is the challenge of ecotourism development in Wondo Genet. Though there is a national tourism policy at federal level, it is very generic lacking detailed action plans that might indicate the ways how to tackle problems and use existing opportunities. 11 per cent each disagree to some extent, remain neutral and agree to some extent about the issue specified as a challenge for the development of ecotourism in Wondo Genet.

Table 6.6.7 Lack of persistent attention and follow-up about tourism development in general and ecotourism development in particular both at national and regional level

		Frequency	Per cent	Valid Per cent	Cumulative Per cent
Valid	Completely Disagree	5	10.0	10.0	10.0
	Disagree to some extent	9	18.0	18.0	28.0
	Neutral/ Don't know	8	16.0	16.0	44.0
	Agree to some extent	13	26.0	26.0	70.0
	Completely Agree	15	30.0	30.0	100.0
	Total	50	100.0	100.0	

Source: Author survey, 2012

Lack of due attention and follow-up about tourism development in general and ecotourism development in particular both at national and regional level is also another challenge of ecotourism development in Wondo Genet since 30 per cent of the respondents completely agree with it and 26 per cent of the respondents agree to some extent about it. On the World Economic Forum (2011) travel and tourism competitiveness index, Ethiopia is ranked 132 out of 139 countries in travel and tourism regulatory framework vividly showing that much has to be done in order to improve the development of travel and tourism in Ethiopia.

Table 6.6.8 Lack of strong and sustainable tourism marketing both at national and regional level

		Frequency	Per cent	Valid Per cent	Cumulative Per cent
Valid	Completely Disagree	8	16.0	16.0	16.0
	Disagree to some extent	5	10.0	10.0	26.0
	2.93	1	2.0	2.0	28.0
	Neutral/ Don't know	7	14.0	14.0	42.0
	Agree to some extent	11	22.0	22.0	64.0
	Completely Agree	18	36.0	36.0	100.0
	Total	50	100.0	100.0	

Source: Author survey, 2012

As the above table depicts 36 per cent of the respondents completely agree that lack of string and sustainable tourism marketing both at national and regional level is the challenge for ecotourism development. 22 per cent agree to some extent with the given statement. On the other hand, 16 per cent of the respondents completely disagree about it and 14 per cent don't know about it.

Table 6.6.9 Difficulty of linking & integrating tourism with other local economies

		Frequency	Per cent	Valid Per cent	Cumulative Per cent
Valid	Completely Disagree	6	12.0	12.0	12.0
	Disagree to some extent	12	24.0	24.0	36.0
	Neutral/ Don't know	6	12.0	12.0	48.0
	Agree to some extent	13	26.0	26.0	74.0
	Completely Agree	13	26.0	26.0	100.0
	Total	50	100.0	100.0	

Source: Author survey, 2012

Problem of creating linkage and integrating tourism with other local economies is one the challenges of ecotourism development in Wondo Genet as 26 per cent each completely agree and agree to some extent regarding the prevalnce of such difficlty. As it is shown in the table, 24 per cent of the respondents disagree to some extent with the statement and 12 per cent each completely disagree and have no idea ablut it.

Table 6.6.10 Failure of creating strong synergy and value chain among various stakeholders that play key roles in the travel and tourism industry

		Frequency	Per cent	Valid Per cent	Cumulative Per cent
Valid	Completely Disagree	4	8.0	8.0	8.0
	Disagree to some extent	5	10.0	10.0	18.0
	Neutral/ Don't know	8	16.0	16.0	34.0
	Agree to some extent	20	40.0	40.0	74.0
	Completely Agree	13	26.0	26.0	100.0
	Total	50	100.0	100.0	

Source: Author survey, 2012

The above table shows that 40 per cent of the respondents agree to some extent that problem of creating strong synergy and value chain among various stakeholders which play key roles in the travel and tourism industry is a challenge for the development of ecotourism in Wondo Genet. 26 per cent of the respondents completely agree about the given statement.

Table 6.6c Statistics

		6.6.11 Absence of incentives, promotions & certifications for those who do care and follow the principles of eco-friendly business development	6.6.12 Difficulty of ensuring the involvement & participation of the community & equity in benefit sharing out of the tourism development	6.6.13 Lack of guideline on how local people could participate & get benefit from ecotourism	6.6.14 Investors giving much focus for short term economic return than environmental sustainability	6.6.15 Mounting pressure and encroachments on the natural resources of the area by the large agrarian neighbourhood surrounding it
N	Valid	50	50	50	50	50
	Missing	0	0	0	0	0
Mean		3.8577	3.6200	3.6800	3.9600	3.9600
Mode		5.00	5.00	5.00	5.00	5.00

Source: Author survey, 2012

Table 6.6.11 Absence of incentives, promotions & certifications for those who do care and follow the principles of eco-friendly business development

		Frequency	Per cent	Valid Per cent	Cumulative Per cent
Valid	Completely Disagree	4	8.0	8.0	8.0
	Disagree to some extent	5	10.0	10.0	18.0
	Neutral/ Don't know	5	10.0	10.0	28.0
	3.69	1	2.0	2.0	30.0
	Agree to some extent	14	28.0	28.0	58.0
	Completely Agree	21	42.0	42.0	100.0
	Total	50	100.0	100.0	

Source: Author survey, 2012

Table 6.6.11 shows that absence of incentives, promotions & certifications for those who do care and follow the principles of eco-friendly business development is a challenge for ecotourism development since 42 per cent and 30 (28% + 2%) per cent of the respondents completely agree and agree to some extent respectively that the stated problem is real in the area. 10 per cent each of the respondents disagree to some extent and don't know about the discription provided. Thus, totally 72 per cent of the respondents agree anyhow that absense of incentives, promotions and certifications for business institutions adhering to the principles of eco-friendly business development is a challenge for the development of ecotourism in Wondo Genet.

6.6.12 Difficulty of ensuring the involvement & equal participation of local community as well as equity in benefit sharing out of tourism development

		Frequency	Per cent	Valid Per cent	Cumulative Per cent
Valid	Completely Disagree	7	14.0	14.0	14.0
	Disagree to some extent	5	10.0	10.0	24.0
	Neutral/ Don't know	5	10.0	10.0	34.0
	Agree to some extent	16	32.0	32.0	66.0
	Completely Agree	17	34.0	34.0	100.0
	Total	50	100.0	100.0	

Source: Author survey, 2012

Difficulty of ensuring the involvement and equal participation of local community as well as equity in benefit sharing out of tourism development is also a challenge for the development of ectourism development in Wondo Genet as 34 per cent and 32 per cent of the respondents completely agree and agree to a certain extent respectively as far as the given issue is concerned. On the other hand, 10 per cent each of the respondents disagree to some extent and remain neutral. Finally, 14 per cent of the respondents completely disagree about the provided problem.

Table 6.6.13. Lack of guideline on how local people could participate & get benefit from ecotourism

		Frequency	Per cent	Valid Per cent	Cumulative Per cent
Valid	Completely Disagree	7	14.0	14.0	14.0
	Disagree to some extent	6	12.0	12.0	26.0
	Neutral/ Don't know	3	6.0	6.0	32.0
	Agree to some extent	14	28.0	28.0	60.0
	Completely Agree	20	40.0	40.0	100.0
	Total	50	100.0	100.0	

Source: Author survey, 2012

As the above table portrays, 40 per cent of the respondents copletely agree that lack of guideline on how local people could participate and get benefit from ecotourism is a challenge to developm ecotourism in Wondo Genet. 28 per cent of the respondents disagree to some extent as well about the statement given. Nevertheless, 14 per cent and 12 per cent of the respondents completely disagree and disagree to some extent that lack of guideline on how local people could participate and get benefit from ecotourism is a challenge to developm ecotourism in Wondo Genet. 6 per cent of the respondents only have taken a neutral position regarding the identified problem.

Table 6.6.14 Investment tendencies giving much focus for short term economic return than environmental sustainability thereby long termand sustainable busienss development

		Frequency	Per cent	Valid Per cent	Cumulative Per cent
Valid	Completely Disagree	5	10.0	10.0	10.0
	Disagree to some extent	3	6.0	6.0	16.0
	Neutral/ Don't know	8	16.0	16.0	32.0
	Agree to some extent	7	14.0	14.0	46.0
	Completely Agree	27	54.0	54.0	100.0
	Total	50	100.0	100.0	

Source: Author survey, 2012

Table 6.6.14 depicts that 54 per cent of the respondents completely agree that investment propensities giving much attention for short term economic benefit than environmental sustainability thereby long termand sustainable busienss development is an other challenge of ecotourism development in the area. 14 per cent of the respondents agree to some extent about it whereas 16 per cent of the respondents stay neutral and 10 per cent completely disagree that Investment tendencies giving much focus for short term economic return is achallenge.

Table 6.6.15 Mounting pressure and encroachments on the natural resources of the area by the large agrarian neighbourhood surrounding it

		Frequency	Per cent	Valid Per cent	Cumulative Per cent
Valid	Completely Disagree	1	2.0	2.0	2.0
	Disagree to some extent	6	12.0	12.0	14.0
	Neutral/ Don't know	8	16.0	16.0	30.0
	Agree to some extent	14	28.0	28.0	58.0
	Completely Agree	21	42.0	42.0	100.0
	Total	50	100.0	100.0	

Source: Author survey, 2012

Eventually, as the above table illustrates, mounting pressure and encroachments on the natural resources of the area by the large agrarian neighbourhood surrounding Wondo Genet is an acute challenge as 42 per cent and 28 per cent of the respondents completely agree and agree to some extent respectively with the given statement. In contrast, 16 per cent of the respondents remain neutral and 12 per cent of the respondents disagree to some extent about it.

6.7 Questions related to public tourism organizations in WG and its surrounding

Table 6.7a Statistics

		6.7.1 Destination management organizations (DMOs, hear after) in the area give capacity building to the local communities	6.7.2 Public tourism organizations empower & engage local people in tourism activities	6.7.3 DMOs in the area conduct awareness creating programs to the local communities and other stakeholders	6.7.4 DMOs do research & investigation about ecotourism development	6.7.5 Public tourism organizations provide financial and support services for communities
N	Valid	50	50	50	50	50
	Missing	0	0	0	0	0
Mean		3.1400	3.5200	3.1200	3.3201	2.8400
Mode		3.00	5.00	2.00	3.00	3.00

Source: Author survey, 2012

Table 6.7.1 Destination management organizations (DMOs, hear after) in the area give capacity building to local communities

		Frequency	Per cent	Valid Per cent	Cumulative Per cent
Valid	Completely Disagree	6	12.0	12.0	12.0
	Disagree to some extent	11	22.0	22.0	34.0
	Neutral/ Don't know	13	26.0	26.0	60.0
	Agree to some extent	10	20.0	20.0	80.0
	Completely Agree	10	20.0	20.0	100.0
	Total	50	100.0	100.0	

Source: Author survey, 2012

The above statement was provided to respondents so as to find out their attitude on the issue specified. As the table indicates 26 per cent of the respondents do not know that Destination Management Organizations (DMOs) in the area provide capacity building to local communities so that they could devise means to get benefited from tourism and ecotourism development. 22

per cent of the respondents disagree to some extent that Destination Management Organizations (DMOs) in the area provide capacity building to local communities. However, 20 per cent each of the respondents completely agree and agree to some extent that Destination Management Organizations (DMOs) in the area provide capacity building to local community thereby they might be involved and benefited from ecotourism development in the area.

Table 6.7.2 Public tourism organizations empower & engage local people in tourism activities

		Frequency	Per cent	Valid Per cent	Cumulative Per cent
Valid	Completely Disagree	4	8.0	8.0	8.0
	Disagree to some extent	9	18.0	18.0	26.0
	Neutral/ Don't know	10	20.0	20.0	46.0
	Agree to some extent	11	22.0	22.0	68.0
	Completely Agree	16	32.0	32.0	100.0
	Total	50	100.0	100.0	

Source: Author survey, 2012

As the above table describes, 32 and 22 per cent of the respondents completely agree and agree to some extent respectively that public tourism organizations empower and engage local people in tourism activities. But, 20 and 18 per cent of the respondents have not idea and disagree to some extent respectively that that public tourism organizations empower and engage local people in tourism activities. Only 8 per cent of the respondents completely disagree about the given explanation.

Table 6.7.3 DMOs in the area conduct awareness creating programs to the local communities and other stakeholders about the advantage and disadvantage of tourism as well as ecotourism.

		Frequency	Per cent	Valid Per cent	Cumulative Per cent
Valid	Completely Disagree	4	8.0	8.0	8.0
	Disagree to some extent	14	28.0	28.0	36.0
	Neutral/ Don't know	14	28.0	28.0	64.0
	Agree to some extent	8	16.0	16.0	80.0
	Completely Agree	10	20.0	20.0	100.0
	Total	50	100.0	100.0	

Source: Author survey, 2012

Table 6.7.3 demonstrates that 28 per cent each of the respondents disagree to a certain extent and have taken a neutral stand respectively that destination Management Orgainizations (DMOs) in the area conduct awareness creation programs to the local communities and other stakeholders about the advantage and disadvantage of tourism as well as ecotourism. Contrary to this, 20 per cent and 16 per cent of the respondnets completely agree and agree to some extent that destination Management Orgainizations (DMOs) in the area conduct awareness creation programs to the local communities and other stakeholders about the advantages and disadvantages of tourism as well as ecotourism.

Table 6.7.4 DMOs do research & investigation about ecotourism development in the area

		Frequency	Per cent	Valid Per cent	Cumulative Per cent
Valid	Completely Disagree	5	10.0	10.0	10.0
	Disagree to some extent	7	14.0	14.0	24.0
	Neutral/ Don't know	15	30.0	30.0	54.0
	3.01	1	2.0	2.0	56.0
	Agree to some extent	11	22.0	22.0	78.0
	Completely Agree	11	22.0	22.0	100.0
	Total	50	100.0	100.0	

Source: Author survey, 2012

The above statement was poised to investigate whether Destination Manegement Organizations do research and investigation about ecotourism development in the area. Unfortunately, 32 per cent of the respondents stay neutral about the issue, yet 22 per cent each completely agree and agree to some extent that DMOs do research and investigation about ecotourism development in the area. Finally, 14 per cent and 10 per cent of the respondents disagree to some extent and completely disagree that DMOs do research and investigation about ecotourism development in Wondo Genet and its surroundings.

Table 6.7.5 Public tourism organizations provide financial and other technical support services for communities

		Frequency	Per cent	Valid Per cent	Cumulative Per cent
Valid	Completely Disagree	9	18.0	18.0	18.0
	Disagree to some extent	11	22.0	22.0	40.0
	Neutral/ Don't know	15	30.0	30.0	70.0
	Agree to some extent	9	18.0	18.0	88.0
	Completely Agree	6	12.0	12.0	100.0
	Total	50	100.0	100.0	

Source: Author survey, 2012

Table 6.7.5 shows that 30 per cent of the respondents don't know that public tourism organizations financial and other technical support services for local communities in the area. 22 per cent and 18 per cent of the respondents disagree to some extent and completely disagree respectively that public tourism organizations financial and other technical support services for local communities in the area. Another 18 per cent and 12 per cent of the respondents agree to some extent and completely agree about the given statement.

Table 6.7b Statistics

		6.7.6 Public tourism organizations do on time inspection and certification duties	6.7.8 Management authorities in the area create conducive environment for private investment
N	Valid	50	50
	Missing	0	0
Mean		2.8305	3.2600
Mode		3.00	4.00

Source: Author survey, 2012

Table 6.7.6 Public tourism organizations do on time inspection and certification duties in Wondo Genet and its surrounding

		Frequency	Per cent	Valid Per cent	Cumulative Per cent
Valid	Completely Disagree	7	14.0	14.0	14.0
	Disagree to some extent	10	20.0	20.0	34.0
	2.53	1	2.0	2.0	36.0
	Neutral/ Don't know	20	40.0	40.0	76.0
	Agree to some extent	8	16.0	16.0	92.0
	Completely Agree	4	8.0	8.0	100.0
	Total	50	100.0	100.0	

Source: Author survey, 2012

As far as the inspection and certification duties of public tourism organizations is concerned, 42 per cent (40% + 2%) of the respondents have taken a neutral position whereas 20 per cent and 14 percent of the respondents completely disagree and disagree to some extent respectively about it. On the other hand, 16 per cent and 8 per cent of the respondents agree to some extent and completely agree respectively that Public tourism organizations do on time inspection and certification duties in Wondo Genet and its surrounding.

Table 6.7.7 Management authorities in the area create conducive environment for private investment

		Frequency	Per cent	Valid Per cent	Cumulative Per cent
Valid	Completely Disagree	4	8.0	8.0	8.0
	Disagree to some extent	10	20.0	20.0	28.0
	Neutral/ Don't know	13	26.0	26.0	54.0
	Agree to some extent	15	30.0	30.0	84.0
	Completely Agree	8	16.0	16.0	100.0
	Total	50	100.0	100.0	

Source: Author survey, 2012

The above table infers 30 per cent of the respondents agree to some extent that management authorities in the area create conducive environment for private investment. Nonetheless, 26 per cent of the respondents remain neutral regarding it and 20 per cent of the respondents disagree to some extent that management authorities in the area create conducive environment for private investment. Lastly, 16 per cent of the respondents completely agree about it whereas 8 per cent of them completely disagree.

6.8 Some questions pertinent to hotels and eco-lodges in WG & its vicinity

Table 6.8a. Statistics

		6.8.1 Eco-lodges use locally produced construction materials as much as possible	6.8.2 There is shortage of locally produced materials for construction of eco-lodges	6.8.3 Most employees in hotels and eco-lodges are from the local area	6.8.4 Eco-lodges use locally produced food items
N	Valid	50	50	50	50
	Missing	0	0	0	0
Mean		3.8149	2.8600	3.6600	3.0800
Mode		5.00	2.00	4.00	4.00

Source: Author survey, 2012

The following tables display some important questions with the corresponding views of respondents regarding the issues provided for them.

Table 6.8.1 Eco-lodges use locally produced construction materials as much as possible

		Frequency	Per cent	Valid Per cent	Cumulative Per cent
Valid	Completely Disagree	3	6.0	6.0	6.0
	Disagree to some extent	7	14.0	14.0	20.0
	Neutral/ Don't know	6	12.0	12.0	32.0
	3.75	1	2.0	2.0	34.0
	Agree to some extent	13	26.0	26.0	60.0
	Completely Agree	20	40.0	40.0	100.0
	Total	50	100.0	100.0	

Source: Author survey, 2012

As table 6.8.1 shows 40 per cent and 28 per cent (26 % + 2%) completely agree and agree to some extent that eco-lodges use locally produced construction materials as much as possible in their construction phase. Using locally produced construction materials is of a great help to reduce the money that leaks out from the local economy. Yet, 14 per cent of the respondents disagree to some extent about the statement. In the end, 12 per cent and 6 per cent of the respondents have no idea and completely disagree that eco-lodges use locally produced construction materials as much as possible in their construction phase.

Table 6.8.2 There is shortage of locally produced materials for construction of eco-lodges

		Frequency	Per cent	Valid Per cent	Cumulative Per cent
Valid	Completely Disagree	9	18.0	18.0	18.0
	Disagree to some extent	15	30.0	30.0	48.0
	Neutral/ Don't know	7	14.0	14.0	62.0
	Agree to some extent	12	24.0	24.0	86.0
	Completely Agree	7	14.0	14.0	100.0
	Total	50	100.0	100.0	

Source: Author survey, 2012

As the above table expresses 30 per cent and 18 per cent of the respondents disagree to some extent and completely disagree respectively about the shortage of locally produced materials for the construction of eco-lodges. However, 24 per cent and 14 per cent of the respondents agree to to some extent and completely agree that there is shortage of locally produced materials for the construction of eco lodges. Moreover, 14 per cent of the respondents don't know about the issue given.

6.8.3 Most employees in hotels and eco-lodges are from the local area

		Frequency	Per cent	Valid Per cent	Cumulative Per cent
Valid	Completely Disagree	2	4.0	4.0	4.0
	Disagree to some extent	8	16.0	16.0	20.0
	Neutral/ Don't know	10	20.0	20.0	40.0
	Agree to some extent	15	30.0	30.0	70.0
	Completely Agree	15	30.0	30.0	100.0
	Total	50	100.0	100.0	

Source: Author survey, 2012

The above question was provided to respondents in order to find out whether hotels and eco-lodges employee locals and as it is shown 30 per cent each completely agree and agree to some extent that most employees in hotels and eco-lodges are from the local area. Only 4 per cent of the respondents completely disagree about it and 16 per cent of the respondents disagree to some extent that most employees in hotels and eco-lodges are from the local area.

Table 6.8.4 Eco-lodges use locally produced food items

		Frequency	Per cent	Valid Per cent	Cumulative Per cent
Valid	Completely Disagree	6	12.0	12.0	12.0
	Disagree to some extent	12	24.0	24.0	36.0
	Neutral/ Don't know	10	20.0	20.0	56.0
	Agree to some extent	16	32.0	32.0	88.0
	Completely Agree	6	12.0	12.0	100.0
	Total	50	100.0	100.0	

Source: Author survey, 2012

As the above table shows 32 per cent and 12 per cent of the respondents agree to some extent and completely agree that eco-lodges use locally produced food items. However, 24 per cent of the respondents disagree to some extent to the issue mentioned. And 20 per cent of them have no idea about it. Finally, 12 per cent of the respondents completely disagree that eco-lodges use locally produced food items.

Table 6.8b Statistics

		6.8.5 Development of lodges are in harmony with their surroundings and the landscape	6.8.6 Hotels sort-out (categorize) their waste materials	6.8.7 Lodges sort-out (Categorize) their waste materials
N	Valid	50	50	50
	Missing	0	0	0
Mean		3.4800	2.7600	2.9198
Mode		5.00	2.00	2.00

Source: Author survey, 2012

Table 6.8.5 Developments of lodges are in harmony with their surroundings and the landscape

		Frequency	Per cent	Valid Per cent	Cumulative Per cent
Valid	Completely Disagree	2	4.0	4.0	4.0
	Disagree to some extent	12	24.0	24.0	28.0
	Neutral/ Don't know	11	22.0	22.0	50.0
	Agree to some extent	10	20.0	20.0	70.0
	Completely Agree	15	30.0	30.0	100.0
	Total	50	100.0	100.0	

Source: Author survey, 2012

Table 6.8.5 elucidates that 30 per cent of the respondents completely agree that the developments of lodges are in harmony with their surroundings and the landscape whereas 24 per cent of them disagree to some extent about the statement. Furthermore, 20 per cent of the respondents agree to some extent that the developments of lodges are in harmony with their surroundings and the landscape. Finally, 22 per cent and 4 per cent of the respondents remain neutral and completely disagree to some extent about the account given respectively. Thus, totally 50 per cent of the respondents agree in any case that the developments of lodges are in harmony with their surroundings and the landscape.

Table 6.8.6 Hotels sort-out (categorize) their waste materials

		Frequency	Per cent	Valid Per cent	Cumulative Per cent
Valid	Completely Disagree	9	18.0	18.0	18.0
	Disagree to some extent	14	28.0	28.0	46.0
	Neutral/ Don't know	12	24.0	24.0	70.0
	Agree to some extent	10	20.0	20.0	90.0
	Completely Agree	5	10.0	10.0	100.0
	Total	50	100.0	100.0	

Source: Author survey, 2012

The above query was provided to examine if hotels sort-out or categorze their waste materials and as the table displays 28 per cent and 24 per cent of the respondents disagree to some extent and have no idea that hotels sort-out or categorze their waste materials respectively. But, 20 per cent and 10 per cent of the respondents agree to some extent and completely agree that hotels categorize or separate their waste materials in and around Wondo Genet. Finally 18 per cent of the respondents completely disagree about it.

Table 6.8.7 Eco-lodges sort-out (categorize) their waste materials

		Frequency	Per cent	Valid Per cent	Cumulative Per cent
Valid	Completely Disagree	9	18.0	18.0	18.0
	Disagree to some extent	12	24.0	24.0	42.0
	Neutral/ Don't know	11	22.0	22.0	64.0
	3.99	1	2.0	2.0	66.0
	Agree to some extent	9	18.0	18.0	84.0
	Completely Agree	8	16.0	16.0	100.0
	Total	50	100.0	100.0	

Source: Author survey, 2012

The above table unveils that 24 per cent and 18 per cent of the respondents disagree to a certain extent and completely disagree respectively that eco-lodges in Wondo Genet and its vicinity sort-out their waste materials. On the other hand, 20 per cent (2% + 18%) and 16 per cent of the respondents agree to some extent and completely agree respectively that eco-lodges sort-out their waste materials. Eventually, 22 per cent of the respondents have taken a neutral position regarding the statement given.

Therefore, on the basis of the overall findings of the study, it could be conceivable to prove or disprove hypothesises proposed earlier. Consequently, the following subtopic is going to verify those propositions stated.

6.9 Hypothesis Testing

Basically, in chapter six, which is the analysis and interpretation section of the research, it could be noticed that the research questions stated in the research problem were assessed and based on the reactions obtained from the respondents, here the researcher would like to verify the propositions or hypothesises tentatively proposed in chapter three of the thesis.

Hypothesis 1: Substandard infrastructural developments are acute challenges of ecotourism development in Wondo Genet as developing destination.

Hypothesis accepted. As the survey outcome vividly exhibits, the vast majority of the respondents asserted that inadequacy and poor infrastructural conditions are the bottlenecks of ecotourism development in Wondo Genet.

Hypothesis2: Unorganized and weak institutional framework is one of the important challenges of ecotourism development in Wondo Genet.

Hypothesis accepted. Again the results of the questionnaire survey reveal that unorganized and weak institutional framework causing to the failure of creating strong synergy and value chain among various stakeholders that play key roles in the travel and tourism industry as well as problems of linking and integrating tourism with other local economies is one of the main challenges of ecotourism development in Wondo Genet.

Hypothesis3: Existence of diverse attractions like pristine natural environments and colourful cultural and historical heritages is a comparative advantage or opportunity of developing destinations.

Hypothesis accepted. This is because the survey result shows that 98 per cent of the respondents to this particular enquiry agree anyhow reaffirming the hypothesis that such resources are essentially the opportunities for developing countries in order to have a competitive tourism industry.

Hypothesis4: Price competitiveness is one of the opportunities for developing ecotourism in Wondo Gent.

Hypothesis accepted. The findings of the analysis, at destination level, and the secondary data from the World Economic Forum (2011), at national level, avowed that price competitiveness (low cost of services and products in the area compared to the international market) is one of the opportunities to develop ecotourism in Wondo Genet.

Chapter Seven

7. Conclusion, Recommendations and Areas of Further Research

7.1 Conclusion

Tourism is a rapidly growing phenomenon and has become one of the largest industries in the world with diverse impacts. It plays a significant and indubitably a positive role in the socio-economic and political development of destination countries in various aspects such as offering new employment opportunities, enabling communities that are poor in material wealth but rich in culture, history, and heritage to use their unique characteristics as an income-generating comparative advantage, stimulating the development of multiple-use infrastructure that benefits the host community, including roads, health care facilities, clean water facilities and sports centres, it also creates networks and linkages among different sectors of the economy, paves the way for cultural understanding and a sense of fraternity and sorority among the people of the world, fuels the creation of small and medium sized local enterprises in a destination, etc. However, unless its development is carefully managed and controlled, it might create various unwanted effects inter alia environmental destruction and pollution, cultural degradation, economic leakage and other social problems like prostitution, drug abuse and conflict as well as tension between tourists and the locals might befall. The fundamental reason why this happens could be due to the varied characteristics and nature of different sorts of tourism development.

Consequently, governments and destination management organizations should be completely aware of the impacts of different forms of tourism development and promote growth models with assumptions and implications that are fully understood.

For instance, a pro-poor tourism approach will seek forms of development that disproportionately benefit the poor (Overseas Development Institute, 2007) likewise ecotourism, which is travel to fragile, pristine, and usually protected areas that strives to be low impact and (often) small scale, helps educate the traveller, provides funds for conservation, directly benefits the economic development and political empowerment of local communities, and fosters respect for different cultures and for human rights (Honey, 2008).

From the existing resource point of view, ecotourism especially is viable to develop it in developing countries. Yet, there are numerous constraints that could curtail the development of ecotourism in least developed countries.

The findings of this study have shown that challenges such as

- ❖ Lack of abundant health facilities,
- ❖ Lack of telecommunication services especially internet banking and internet services, technological limitations in waste treatment and recycling,
- ❖ Absence of clear guidelines which can push hoteliers and other establishments to reduce energy and water consumption,
- ❖ Lack of awareness towards cleaner production and eco-friendly business ethics,
- ❖ Absence of strategic policy framework and environmental code of ethics specifically addressing issues related to ecotourism development,
- ❖ Lack of persistent attention and follow-up about tourism development in general and ecotourism development in particular both at national and regional level,
- ❖ Lack of strong and sustainable tourism marketing both at national and regional level,
- ❖ Difficulty of linking and integrating tourism with other local economies,
- ❖ Difficulty of creating strong synergy and value chain among various stakeholders that play key roles in the travel and tourism industry,
- ❖ Absence of incentives, promotions and certifications for those who do care and follow the principles of eco-friendly business development,
- ❖ Difficulty of ensuring the involvement and equal participation of local community as well as equity in benefit sharing out of tourism development,
- ❖ Lack of guideline on how local people could participate and get benefit from ecotourism, Investment tendencies giving much focus for short term economic return than environmental sustainability thereby long term and sustainable business development and
- ❖ Mounting pressure and encroachments on the natural resources of the area by the large agrarian neighbourhood surrounding Wondo Genet are the most pertinent challenges of ecotourism development in the area.

On the other hand, there are a number of opportunities of ecotourism development in Wondo Genet, Southern Ethiopia, among them the

- ❖ Presence of supportive rules and regulations from the government,
- ❖ The availability of adequate number of trained manpower in the field,
- ❖ Existence of diverse tourist attraction spots and places of special interest,
- ❖ The hospitality and friendliness of the local population,
- ❖ Existence of natural hot springs which can add value for the normal tourist products,

- ❖ Strategic location and conducive weather factors, and
- ❖ Price competitiveness in travel and tourism can be mentioned.

The survey collected from respondents affirmed that Wondo Genet could be well regarded as the right place for tourism development mainly from its tourism resources view point particularly for the development of community based ecotourism, tourism related to cultural and historical attractions, commercial and recreational tourism as well as wellness and health tourism (Spa and therapy related tourism).

Different literatures have proved that tourism; particularly ecotourism, can be used as an instrument towards local sustainable development. According to the United Nations Conference on Trade and Development UNCTAD/WTO 2009, there are so many different places in the tourism economy where poor people can participate. It is important to think about where they could participate directly in tourism, and also indirectly. As long as the direct participation is concerned, poor and local people might provide goods and services directly to tourists. For instance, they may work in a hotel or restaurant, sell crafts on the pavement, run rickshaws or boats for tourists, or host them in their village. On the other hand, the local community could participate in tourism indirectly through working in those sectors that supply the tourism industry. For example, they may grow and sell vegetables that are served up in tourist hotels, or work for the construction or soft furnishing sectors which provide its services for the hotels. Looking deep in to the core concept of ecotourism as the International Ecotourism Society (TIES) define it "a responsible travel to natural areas that conserves the environment and improves the well-being of local people" (TIES, 2010), acting responsibly in a destination in order to conserve the environment and the improvement of the well-being of the local people must be given a due attention. Therefore, if the principles of ecotourism which demand to function in harmony with the environment, economic, social and cultural pillars are implemented appropriately, ecotourism could be used as a driver for the sustainable development of the local destination. Meaning, ecotourism strongly advocates the participation of the local community directly or in directly in the tourism industry, promotes the development of tourism businesses in harmony with the destination and the landscape, encourages the use of locally produced inputs and supplies in hotels, lodges, ecolodges and so on and strongly backs the creation of strong value chains among the dispersed tourism and other related sectors.

7.2 Recommendations

Regarding safety and security in and around Wondo Genet, the findings show a positive outcome. But yet, much has to be done since security and political stability are key factors in building a positive country image and attracting foreign and domestic investment for tourism development. Especially in post-conflict countries the perception of risk may be disproportionate to actual conditions. From this point of view, Ethiopia has not a positive image due to bloody 17 years civil wars in 1970s and 1980s and destructive wars with Eritrea from 1998 to 2000. Moreover, the current hostile relation with Eritrea and the precarious situation in Somalia do need a special attention and cross border security must be adequately safeguarded. Thus issues related to security must be sufficiently addressed and it is well-known that safety is a prerequisite for existence and survival of tourism.

Another important issue to be taken in to consideration is the environmental quality and purity of Wondo Genet and its vicinity. Generally, 96 per cent of the respondents confirmed that the environmental quality and purity of the area is stunning. However, as future destination of ecotourism niche market, this scenario ought to be further reinforced and sustained. This is due to the reason that tourism itself, not to mention ecotourism, is chiefly depend on the quality of the environment in a given destination.

Respondents of the questionnaire survey asserted that there is lack of adequate shops (all regular shops, gift and craft shops) in the area leading to low tourist spending per day which in turn negatively affects the economic contribution of tourism in the area. Consequently, the destination management organizations in the area should solve this problem through providing various incentives and skill development together with awareness creation to the local community so that they could involve themselves in those sectors. It could be possible to unite the local community and establish a community owned tourism enterprise that might operate in the above mentioned areas including accommodation, transportation and entertainment sectors. That way it is certainly possible to create an opportunity for the local community to get equitable benefit from the tourism development in the area and attain one of the core principles of ecotourism.

As the results of the study illuminate, there is a problem of linking and integrating tourism with other local economies as well as creating a strong synergy and value chain among various tourism stakeholders in and around Wondo Genet area. This is definitely a major setback for the positive contribution of tourism in general and ecotourism specifically in the destination. Thus, such difficulties need to be eliminated as soon as possible in order to maximize the role of ecotourism in the overall local economy.

As long as the kind of tourism very compatible to develop in Wondo Genet is regarded, it might be very crucial to pay a special emphasis on community based ecotourism, wellness and health related tourism and tourism related to cultural and historical attractions respectively as the outcomes of the questionnaire survey indicate. This final remark stated actually on the basis of existing tourism resources in the area. Thus, destination management organizations and any other concerned public tourism organizations should enlighten and make the investment environment very welcoming to those investors who would like to involve themselves in private business development in the area.

Earlier studies have proven that many of the wild animals, birds and vegetation species are endangered and even some of them already have vanished in Wondo Genet. Hence, protecting and rescuing these species is fundamentally significant. Among many measures, developing ecotourism in the area could be one remedy. Therefore, the proper development of ecotourism in and around Wondo Genet has a multiplied vantage.

Rules and regulations from the national and regional government are somehow supportive according to the result of the study. Yet, based on the World Economic Forum (2011) competitiveness report, Ethiopia as a country is placed 132 out of 139 countries on policy rules and regulations, which shows a very poor performance. Thus, a lot has to done towards the improvement of the travel and tourism regulatory framework.

The availability of adequate number of trained manpower in the field (tourism) is one of the opportunities of ecotourism development in Wondo Genet according to the feedbacks generated from respondents. Although this is true, studies proven that the tourism sector is very indigenous where almost all the tourist product is owned, managed and staffed by Ethiopian nationals (Mitchell & Coles, 2009). While this is positive in the sense of minimising economic leakages it is also means that managers in the sector may be simply unaware of international service levels. Hence, ways should be facilitated to gain international exposures and experiences since the tourism market is becoming very competitive from time to time across the globe.

International tourism has been growing in emerging and developing markets over the past decade. This is also true for ecotourism in those emerging destinations. The respondents incorporated in the survey also agree that the growing trend of international ecotourism demand is one the opportunities to develop ecotourism at grassroots level in Wondo Genet. The case of Ethiopia is even very favourable in terms of the profile of international tourists visiting Ethiopia for mainly cultural, heritage and historical reasons. A study funded by The World Bank (2006) outlined that the majority of visitors to Ethiopia are from the post-family and retired life stages (typical age group 50 to 60, no dependent children, well-travelled, Well-educated, sensitive to environmental and social concerns, and take holidays in off-peak periods). Price is cited as a constraint for younger people, although the Omo Valley does tend to attract a slightly younger visitor from the pre-family life-stage. Consequently, the above mentioned tourists are exactly corresponded with the behaviour and characteristics of ecotourists so that the question of potential and target markets is not so pertinent and just it is a matter of using them as ecotourists.

Incentivising, promoting and certifying those business establishments who do care and adhere the principles of eco-friendly business ethics is of profound significance. Unfortunately, such actions are not customary in Wondo Genet and its environs. Hence, it would be so vital to give incentives, publicity and certification business entities which function in harmony with the notion and core principles of ecotourism.

One of the basic features of ecotourism is providing opportunities for local people to participate and get advantage of the tourism development. Nevertheless, due to lack of clear guidelines on how local people could participate and get benefited from ecotourism, this objective is highly disregarded. Thus, designing well-articulated guidelines specifying the procedures and steps of local participation and involvement is very imperative.

The result of the survey also reveals that the intent of many investors in the area is short term economic return than environmental sustainability thereby sustainable and eco-friendly tourism business development. Therefore, influential work has to be done to revert this scenario in the destination.

As far as the problems related to encroachments and pressures from the neighbourhood agrarian community is concerned, both short term long term solutions should be designed. In fact finding out solutions for those matters needs other scrutinized studies. Nonetheless, transforming their traditional method of crop production and livestock rearing through the introduction of modern technology could be used as a short term remedy whereas voluntary resettlement to another area might be considered as a long term solution to curb those problems.

As the outcomes of the survey result show DMOs in the area do not conduct awareness creating programs to the local communities and other stakeholders about the advantage and disadvantage of tourism as well as ecotourism. Thus, it could be very unlikely that the local communities could understand about the pros and cons of tourism resulting inability to minimize the negative impacts and positive effects of tourism in the area. Accordingly, it would be very fine if DMOs in the area do the aforementioned duties so as to create full awareness all about tourism and ecotourism.

Carrying out research and investigation about ecotourism development in the area as well as providing financial and other technical support services for local communities to point out the rooms for involvement and encourage participation are also vital tasks of public tourism and destination management organizations there in Wondo Genet and its environs. Yet, the results of the study do not show a positive trend uncovering limitations in these aspects. So it should be taken in to consideration that performing the above mentioned tasks are of paramount significance for the development of ecotourism and virtuous involvement of local communities.

Lodges and ecolodges in the area have been using locally produced construction materials as much as possible and most of the employees there are from the local area as the findings of the research have shown. This is certainly a good signal which ought to be further strengthened.

Finally, another supportable cultures found out in the study are the tendency of developing lodges in harmony with their surroundings and the landscape as well as using locally produced food items for their consumption. However, much more has to be done in respect to proper waste disposal and categorization all in ecolodges, lodges and hotels found in the area as the results of the study vividly unveil.

7.3 Areas of Further Research

It was very fundamental to investigate the challenges and opportunities of ecotourism development in Wondo Genet, Southern Ethiopia. This is because; to date generally tourism and particularly ecotourism as well as sustainable tourism development could be labelled yet in the stage of exploration in Ethiopian perspective. Hence there is an ample room for the development of tourism in a sustainable and eco-friendly manner from the very beginning. But, it sounds so vital to assess what sorts of constraints and prospects precisely are there in the area prior to the development of the aforementioned types of tourism. Therefore, this study tried to find out the main challenges and opportunities of ecotourism development in Wondo Genet as it is expounded in the problem description.

Nevertheless, it would be significant to further breakdown the problem in to specific areas and conduct another research. For instance, problems such as how to solve the problem of public encroachments and pressures on Wondo Genet, what kinds of incentives and encouragements should be done for investors so that they could participate in tourism investment in the area in order to alleviate lack of tourism facilities, what mechanisms should be designed so as to fully involve locals and equitably distribute all benefits that accrue out from ecotourism development are some of the areas of future research the researcher would like to mention.

Eventually, as the author of the study, I would like to underline my strong desire and aspiration to continue further my study to PhD level in areas related to ecotourism and its role for sustainable livelihood development from developing countries perspective. Likewise, issues such as sustainable tourism development, tourism economics, customer care and service quality management are my areas of interest for a PhD study in the future.

--------------/////////--------------

References

Ali, M. (2007). Recreation Use Value of Wondo Genet Wetland Ecosystem- Ethiopia. Master Thesis submitted to the Department of Forest Resources Management at Saint Louis University in partial fulfilment of the requirements for the degree of Master of Science.

Christie, T., Crompton, E. (2001). Tourism in Africa. Africa Region Working Paper Series by the World Bank

Cross, P. (2003). The Butterflies of Wondo Genet: An Introduction to the Butterflies of

Endawoke, Y. (2011). Research Methods for Tourism Management Students. Bahirdar

Erlet, C. (1993). Ecotourism in the third world: Problems for sustainable tourism development. *Tourism Management, 14(2),* 85-90.

Esen, S. (2010). Competitiveness of tourism and the evaluation of Turkey according to international tourism competitiveness criteria, Bartin University, Faculty of Economics and Administrative Sciences, Turkey

Ethiopia: In Makeda's Footsteps (2006). Towards a Strategy for Pro-Poor Tourism Development Prepared for the Government of Ethiopia by The World Bank,Ethiopia. Addis Ababa.

Federal Democratic Republic of Ethiopia Population Census Commission, (2007). Summary and Statistical Report of the Population and Housing Census, Addis Ababa

Gemechu, T. (2005). Prospects of Sustainable Natural Resource Management andLivelihood Development in Wondo Genet Area, Southern Ethiopia. A Thesis Submitted to the School of Graduate Studies of Addis Ababa University in partial Fulfilment for the Degree of Masters of Arts in Regional and Local Development Studies

Goeldner, R., & Ritchie, B. (2009). Tourism, principles, practices philosophy. 11th edn, New Jersey, USA, John Willey &Sons Inc.

Higham, J. (2007). Critical Issues in Ecotourism: understanding a complex tourism phenomenon, Elsevier Ltd, Amsterdam

Honey, M & Gilpin, R. (2009). Tourism in the Developing World: Promoting Peace and Reducing Poverty. Special report 233, Washington

Honey, M. (2008). Ecotourism and Sustainable Development: Who owns the paradise? Island press, Washington DC, USA

Inskeep, E. (1991). Tourism Planning: An Integrated and Sustainable Development Approach, John Wily and Sons Inc, New York, USA

IUCN (2011). Tourism and the Environment. http://data.iucn.org/dbtw-wpd/html/Tourism [*www document, accessed 21/02/12*]

Jamieson, W (2006). Community Destination Management in Developing Economies. Howorth press, Inc. New York

Jonathan Mitchell, J. & Christopher Coles, C. (2009). Enhancing private sector and community engagement in tourism services in Ethiopia, Overseas Development Institute

Khanal, R, & Babar, T (2007). Community Based Ecotourism for Sustainable Tourism Development in the Mekong Region, published by CUTS Hanoi Resource Centre, 81 Chua Lang Street, Dong Da District, Hanoi, Vietnam,

Lincoln, Y. S., & Guba, E., G. (2000). Paradigmatic controversies, contradictions and emerging confluences. *Handbook of Qualitative Research (2nd edn, 163-188)*. Thousand Oaks, CA: Sage Publications, Inc.

Lonely Planet (2009). Ethiopia & Eritrea - Southern Ethiopia Chapter, 4th edn.

McIntosh, R. & Goeldner, C. (1990). Tourism, principles, practices philosophy. 6th edn, New York, USA, John Willey &Sons Inc.

Mihalic, T. (2006). Tourism and its Environments. Economic, Ecological and Political Sustainability Issues. Ljubljana, Slovenia

Ministry of Culture and Tourism, (2009). FederalDemocratic Republic of Ethiopia Tourism Development Policy, Addis Ababa, Ethiopia

Mitchell, J., Ashely, C. (2010). Tourism and poverty reduction pathways to prosperity. Overseas Development Institute, London UK

Nathy, Y. (2010). Ecotourism and sustainability: opportunities and challenges in the case of Nepal, Master thesis, department of sustainable development, University of Uppsala, Sweden

NCAP, (2007). Poverty Reduction at Risk in Ethiopia: An Assessment of the Impacts of Climate Change on Poverty Alleviation Activities

Ngunyi, N, (2009). Ecotourism and Sustainable Development in Kenya, Sun YatSen University, Doctoral Thesis.

Overseas Development Institute (2007). Briefing Paper: Can tourism offer pro-poor pathways to prosperity? Examining evidence on the impact of tourism on poverty.

Paul, D. (2009). A history of the concept of sustainable development. University of Oradea, Faculty of Economics Volger, J. (2007). The international politics of sustainable development. Published in the handbook of sustainable development, Edward Elgar Publishing Ltd, Cheltenham

Payne, D., & Raiborn, C. (2001). Sustainable development: the ethic support the economics, journal of business ethics 32(2), 157-168

Pedersen, A. (1991). Issues, problems, and lessons learned from ecotourism planning projects. In: J. Kusler (Ed.), *Ecotourism and resource conservation* (61-74). Selected papers from the 2nd International Symposium: Ecotourism and Resource Conservation, Madison: Omnipress.

Peter U.C. Dieke, (2003) "Tourism in Africa's economic development: policy implications", *Management Decision, 41* (3), 287 – 295

Quebec Declaration on Ecotourism, 2002, Quebec, Canada. http://www.gdrc.org/uem/eco-tour/quebec-declaration.pdf [*www document, accessed 20/02/2012*]

Ramona, F. & Gabriela, C. (2010). Relationship between Tourism and Sustainable Development in the European Context, the Centre of European Studies

Ramser, T. (2007). Evaluating Ecotourism in Laikipia, Kenya. A Master Thesis submitted to the Faculty of Natural Sciences, University of Bern

Report of the World Tourism Organization to the United Nations Secretary-General in preparation for the High Level Meeting on the Mid-Term Comprehensive Global Review of the Programme of Action for the Least Developed Countries for the Decade 2001-2010

Ross, S,.& Wall, G. (1999). Ecotourism: Towards congruence between theory and practice, Faculty of Environmental Studies, University of Waterloo, 200 University Avenue West, Waterloo, Ont, Canada N2L 3G1

Self, M., Self, R. & Haynes, B. (2010). Marketing tourism in the Galapagos Islands: Ecotourism or green washing? International business and economics research journal 9(6), 1-16

Shrestha, B. (2009). Research Paradigms: An Overview. Teaching material for Master's Program in Renewable Energy, Department of Mechanical Engineering, Institute of Engineering, Nepal

Singh, J. (2010). Ecotourism, I.K International Publishing House, New Delhi, India

Stem, C., Lassoie, J., Lee, D., Deshler, D., & Schelhas, J. (2003). Community participation in ecotourism benefits: The link to conservation practices and perspectives. Society Natural Resources, 16(5), 387-413

Teklay, T. (2005). Organic inputs from agroforestry trees on-farms for improving soil quality and crop productivity in Ethiopia, Doctoral thesis, Faculty of Forest Sciences, Department of Forest Ecology, Umeå

The International Ecotourism Society. (2010). Washington DC, USA

TIES, (2006). TIES Global Ecotourism Fact Sheet, USA, Washington

Tiffany M. Doan (2000): The Effects of Ecotourism in Developing Nations: An Analysis of Case Studies, *Journal of Sustainable Tourism, 8:4, 288-304*

UNDP (2011). Tourism and poverty reduction strategies in the integrated framework for least developed countries

UNWTO, (2004). Indicators of sustainable development for tourism destinations. A guidebook. - Madrid.

UNWTO, (2011). Tourism Highlights. Madrid, Spain

UNWTO, (2012). Why Tourism? http://www2.unwto.org/en/content/why-tourism [*www document, accessed 21/02/2012*]

Waver, D. (2006) *Sustainable Tourism: Theory and Practice.* Elsevier Ltd

WEF, (2011). The Travel & Tourism Competitiveness Report. Geneva, Switzerland

Wood, E. (2002). Ecotourism, its principles and practices and policies for Sustainability, UNEP division of technology, industry and economics

World Bank, (2006). Ethiopia: Towards a strategy for pro-poor tourism development

WTTC, (2012). Travel & Tourism Economic Impact: Ethiopia. London, United Kingdom

Yabebal, M. (2010). Tourist Flows and Its Determinants in Ethiopia. Ethiopian Development Research Institute, Addis Ababa.

i want morebooks!

Buy your books fast and straightforward online - at one of world's fastest growing online book stores! Environmentally sound due to Print-on-Demand technologies.

Buy your books online at
www.get-morebooks.com

Kaufen Sie Ihre Bücher schnell und unkompliziert online – auf einer der am schnellsten wachsenden Buchhandelsplattformen weltweit! Dank Print-On-Demand umwelt- und ressourcenschonend produziert.

Bücher schneller online kaufen
www.morebooks.de

VDM Verlagsservicegesellschaft mbH
Heinrich-Böcking-Str. 6-8   Telefon: +49 681 3720 174   info@vdm-vsg.de
D - 66121 Saarbrücken   Telefax: +49 681 3720 1749   www.vdm-vsg.de

Lightning Source UK Ltd.
Milton Keynes UK
UKHW012350210421
382415UK00001B/53